SPECTRES OF CAPITALISM

A Critique of Current Intellectual Fashions

SPECTRES OF CAPITALISM

A Critique of Current Intellectual Fashions

SAMIR AMIN

TRANSLATED BY SHANE HENRY MAGE

Monthly Review Press
New York

Library of Congress Cataloging-in-Publication Data

Amin, Samir.
   [Au-delà du capitalisme. English]
   Spectres of capitalism: a critique of current intellectual
   fashions / by Samir Amin; translated, Shane Henry Mage.
         p. cm.
   Translation of: Au-delà du capitalisme.
   Includes bibliographical references (p. 147) and index.
   ISBN 0-85345-934-7 (cloth). — ISBN 0-85345-933-9 (paper)
   1. Capitalism. 2. Economic history. 3. Social history.
4. Postmodernism. I. Title.
HB501.A586513   1998
330. 12'2—dc21   98-9578
                                                        CIP

Monthly Review Press
122 West 27th Street
New York, NY 10001

Manufactured in the United States of America
10 9 8 7 6 5 4 3 2 1

Contents

Introduction

For the last century and a half, the spectre of communism has been haunting the world. Like any other spectre it can never be suppressed once and for all, even though it often happens that those fearing its menace are able, for a while, to get it out of their minds. And at each of those times they repeat the same orgiastic spectacle of gluttons falling over each other to grab even more riches, to gorge themselves on even more extra helpings from the table, and to take whatever drugs they hope will relieve their indigestion. They all repeat in chorus the same catch-phrases: "Marx is dead," "History has reached the end of its voyage, and nothing will ever again change," "Here we are, and here we stay for evermore!" Some really believe that their dream world will last to all eternity. Others, troubled despite everything by a slight inquietude, look around themselves and murmur, "We really have to do *something* for everyone we keep away from our party: perhaps we should hand out some scraps from our feast to those poor souls." Meanwhile, among the innumerable victims there are those who cry over their fate, those who take refuge in ever-repeated tales of their glorious struggles in the past but who understand nothing of the causes for their recent defeats, and those who resign themselves to their condition and think, "God is with our enemies, there is nothing to do but hope for a softening of their hearts while we huddle at the fence over which they toss their leavings." But there are also some who calmly call for a meeting of those who can analyze the new situation, take the measure of the strengths and weaknesses of both camps, understand the challenges confronting their peoples, and in this way prepare for tomorrow's struggles and victories.

One hundred fifty years after the *Communist Manifesto* was put forth, we are once again in one of those moments when the gluttons hold their orgy. But this momentary triumph of unrestrained capital is not accompanied by a brilliant new expansive surge for capitalism but by the deepening of its crisis! Thus, the boundless appetite of capital, given full scope by the momentary weakening of its adversary class, in fact shows explosively the absurd irrationality of this system. The inequality that it promotes undermines its possibilities for expansion. It expands consumption in a distorted manner by favoring wholesale waste by the rich, but this in no way compensates for the poverty to which it condemns the majority of workers and peoples, who become ever less successfully integrated into its system of exploitation. So capitalism, by its very logic, reduces them to a marginal status and settles for mere crisis management, which it can do just as long as the social power of its adversaries is not reconstituted. This paradoxical victory of capital giving rise to its prolonged crisis is only apparent if we cool off by reading the *Communist Manifesto* and recall to our memory the plain reason for this: capitalism is incapable of overcoming its fundamental contradictions.

To destroy the conquests of the working classes, to dismantle the systems of social security and employment protection, to return to poverty wages, to bring certain of the peripheral countries back to their outmoded status as providers of raw materials while limiting the opportunities of those who have become relatively industrialized by imposing the status of subcontractor on their productive systems, and to speed up the squandering of the resources of the planet: such is the program of the currently dominant forces. This permanently reactionary utopia expresses the deepest desire of the gluttons whose arrogant self-affirmation bursts out all over at historical moments like our present one.

The critique of current intellectual fashions that I put forth in this contribution to the sesquicentennial of the *Communist Manifesto* will accentuate the nullity of this reactionary utopia.

In the first place, its scientific nullity, nullity of this "pure economics" which claims for itself the title "neoclassical," even though it stands at the opposite pole from the method of classical economics and which applies itself laboriously to the task of proving what can never be proved: that markets are self-regulating in a way that produces a natural, general equilibrium which is the best possible for society. Marx, free from the morbid preoccupation of bourgeois ideologies (which is to legitimize capitalist society through declaring it definitively unsurpassable, the End of History) reminds us simply that to believe in a natural equilibrium governing society is to believe in something absurd, which can be sought only in blind alleys. In place of this false question Marx poses the real task, which is to analyze the contradictions of the system, those which define its historical limits. A rereading of the *Manifesto*, in today's world, makes apparent immediately and convincingly the superiority of Marx's century-and-a-half-old analysis. It remains closer to today's reality than all the neoliberal effusions of an economics that goes whichever way the wind blows. And that empty economics has its pale complement in the enfeebled social and philosophical theses of "postmodernism," which teach us to be happy and to cope with the system on a day-to-day basis, while closing our eyes to the ever more gigantic catastrophes which it is cooking up for us. Postmodernism thus legitimizes, in its own way, the manipulative practices required of political managers for whom democracy must be reduced to the status of a "low intensity" activity even as it treats the attachment of a society to its own identity as something neurotic, empty, and impotent.

This contribution is likewise offered in the hope that, starting from this analysis of the weaknesses of our apparently triumphant enemy, we will size up what is objectively required for a humanist answer to the challenge. This answer, today, takes on an even more pressing necessity than it did one hundred fifty years ago. The socialization of labor, on an immeasurably greater scale than in 1848, has put on the agenda the withering away of the law of value. Capitalism's short-run rationality, by its incompetence to put forward acceptable means for managing the future of our planet, is now producing destructive effects unimaginable a century and a half ago. Since the time of the *Manifesto*, polarization on a world scale has taken on a scope unparalleled in all previous history. This forces us, in looking to reconcile the universalist dimension of the human enterprise with respect for the diversity of the peoples undertaking that enterprise, to do so by means surpassing those that bourgeois thought has been able to conceive and by methods that go outside the logic that sets what bourgeois thought accepts as practical.

These questions, old ones, though rephrased by the challenges posed by their historical development, ask that we do not reread the *Manifesto* as if it were a sacred (which to me means dead, even embalmed) text. Rather, the spirit of this text, which was so far ahead of its time that whole paragraphs of it can be quoted as if written yesterday, must be an invitation to us to continue its still unfinished task.

History has proven that capitalism, like all social systems, is able at each stage of its expansion to overcome its own permanent contradictions, but not without worsening the violence with which they will be experienced by succeeding generations. This is not at all foreign to the Marxian spirit, which I express in the proposition that the human enterprise remains underdetermined, that it is not foreclosed by some necessity that is tied to the development of either the productive forces or any other metasocial force. More than ever humanity is confronted with two choices: to let itself be led by capitalism's unfolding logic to a fate of collective suicide or, on the contrary, to give birth to the enormous human possibilities carried by that world-haunting spectre of communism.

1

Capitalist Crisis and the Crisis of Capitalism

I

No social phenomenon unfolds in a regular, continuous, and unlimited manner. The evolution of any society thus necessarily goes through phases of expansion, stagnation, and even regression. The points at which there is a change of direction are then termed crises. This general concept applies to all societies throughout history, and it is valid for all aspects of social life, whether economic, political, or cultural. Taken in this broad sense, any conceptual discussion of crises, like discussion of social evolution as such, is part of the subject matter of the philosophy of history. Our present consideration deals only with the concept of economic crisis specific to the modern capitalist system, thus taking up a very limited portion of this domain of thought.

The adjective "economic" expresses the major transformation introduced by capitalism: it gives a dominant position to the economic dimension, as opposed to the dominance of political and ideological dimensions in previous systems. This reversal in the order of things can be expressed by saying that under capitalism wealth is the source of power while under previous systems the reverse was the case. Or, to put it another way, the law of value governs not only the economic aspect of capitalism but all aspects of its social life.

This sort of capitalism took on its finished form only with the industrial revolution—starting, say, in 1800. From that time onward the social contradiction immanent in the capitalist mode of production has involved a permanent tendency of the system to "produce more than can be consumed": downward pressure on wages has tended to generate a volume of profits which, under competitive forces, flow into a volume of investment relatively in excess of the investment level required to satisfy the effective demand for the system's products. From this viewpoint, the threat of relative stagnation is the chronic ailment of capitalism. Crises and depressions do not need to be explained by specific causes. On the contrary, it is the expansion phases that are each produced by their own particular circumstances.

This specific characteristic of modern capitalism cannot be projected backward, neither to the long transition to capitalism—the three centuries of mercantilism from 1500 to 1800—nor, a fortiori, to still earlier epochs. The cycles, expansions, crises, and depressions of the mercantilist transition are thus part of a specific set of problems, different from the set of problems characteristic of full capitalism. Here we will be discussing only the concept of economic crisis appropriate to full capitalism.

The history since 1800 of "really existing capitalism" is the history of a prodigious development of productive forces, unparalleled in earlier epochs. The tendency to stagnate inherent in capitalism has thus been overcome time and again. A necessary condition for understanding this fact is to integrate, in a single overall explanation, the economic mechanisms and the social and political struggles which structure the operations of crisis, both on the scale of national formations and on that of the worldwide capitalist system. It then becomes possible to put forward theories governing the type of capital accumulation proper to each significant phase discernible in this historical epoch. This is done on the basis of theories dealing with the state, the hegemonic social relations that make up its mode of existence, and its international relations of rivalry and supremacy, dominance and dependency, all tied into theories of macroeconomic equilibria and disequilibria in the realms of supply and demand, as well by the balance among global and sectoral interests. These theories are to explain the causes and mechanisms of economic expansions, the causes of their exhaustion, and, accordingly, the specific nature of the crisis through which each expansion is terminated, as well as the stakes of the struggles and structural changes which, once the crisis is over, create the conditions for a new expansion.

These analyses and theories of crisis can be applied at three main levels, generally referred to as *short-term business cycle*, *long wave*, and *general* or *fundamental systemic crisis*.

II

The *short-term business cycle* consists of alternating phases of expansion and recession, the whole cycle extending over several years.

Equipped with the conceptual toolbox of economic science, we can easily enough set up an economic model that internally generates a monotonic cycle by bringing into play the two well-known mechanisms of the multiplier (an addition to personal income when spent on consumption gives rise to a secondary series of derived incomes) and the accelerator (the increased demand stemming from increased incomes gives rise to increased investment spending).

This model can be improved by adding to it the induced cyclical variations of interest rates and of relative changes in real wages and profits. It can be expressed in the framework of a closed or open national economy, or in that of the global economy. It can be equally well formulated in the purely empirical terms of conventional economics or in those of the Marxian law of value. All these exercises in economics, or in political economy, are expressed in the rigorously abstract framework of the capitalist mode of production, which is the necessary and sufficient condition for their validity. It is interesting to note that the results obtained in this way give a good skeletal account of the short-term business cycle (around seven years long, on average) that in actual fact marked the long century from 1815 to 1945. After the Second World War, the business cycle seems to have become subject to a greater degree of control, thanks to more activist state intervention and controls over borrowing, interest rates, income distribution, public spending, and so forth. (Similarly, and just as easily, it is possible to set up models of shorter-term fluctuations, centering on the inventory cycle, which correspond equally well to the real sequences of economic activity under modern industrial capitalism.)

That these economic models worked well for nearly a century and a half in describing real economic fluctuations is due to the existence, specific to that period, of a governing mechanism marked by several noteworthy features: (a) regulation of competition among enterprises through upward and downward pressures on the wage-level (and this type of regulation applies equally to both the phase of competitive capitalism from 1800 to 1880, and the phase of oligopolistic capitalism that followed it); (b) relative stability in the social structures of dominance within each of the main national formations; (c) national administration of the system through internal control of money supply and interest rates;

(d) stability in the distinction, established in this period and constantly deepened throughout it, between the industrialized centers and an unindustrialized periphery.

But ever since the end of the Second World War, when regulation of the system by competition gave way to a historical compromise between capital and labor, which provided the basis for Keynesianism and the welfare state, and when the peripheral areas began to compete in industrial production, the regular periodic movement of the business cycle gave way to a shorter, more smoothed-out, but also more irregular cycle.

III

Beyond the cyclical analysis put forward here in strictly economic terms, the study of long waves requires us to broaden our conceptual horizon in order to include all the dimensions of historical materialism.

For the whole period following the industrial revolution we can actually, in the area defined strictly in terms of conventional economics (production, investment, prices, incomes), discern such "long waves" (usually called Kondratiev cycles). In fact, price indexes show a falling tendency from 1815 to 1850, a rising tendency from 1850 to 1865, a falling tendency from 1865 to 1900, and a rising tendency from 1900 to 1914. However, the most persuasive explanation has nothing to do with the concept of a cycle as such. As a matter of fact the turning points at 1850 and 1900 coincide with the bringing into production of vast new gold reserves in North America and then South Africa. The monetary system prevailing from 1815 to 1914 was based on a simple gold standard, and in that system the long-term evolution of the nominal price level was governed by a falling tendency due to steady increases in the productivity of labor. This tendency was subject to counteraction by occasional increases in the productivity of gold-mining labor, which took place abruptly in the California gold rush of 1850 and the Klondike and Rand gold rushes of 1900. But the price increases resulting from these gold inflows ran out of steam within fifteen years, allowing the long-run falling tendency of the price level to resume its preponderant influence.

It is not necessary to adopt one or another theory of cycles in order to investigate those long cycles that apply to the rate of growth of real output and, necessarily, to that of capital investment. In this regard, we note the following four waves, each of about a half century in duration:

1790-1814 Expansion	1814-1848 Slump
1848-1872 Expansion	1872-1893 Slump
1893-1914 Expansion	1914-1945 Slump
1945-1968 Expansion	1968- Slump

One can scarcely fail to notice that each successive expansion phase corresponds quite exactly to a combination of major technological innovations and market-expanding political developments. These are, successively, (a) the first industrial revolution, with the French Revolution and the violent growth of an empire; (b) the construction of a full railroad network, with Italian and German unification; (c) electrification, with colonialist imperialism; and (d) postwar reconstruction and modernization of Europe and Japan, with the emergence of "automobile civilization."

To put it another way, there is no room for an artificial separation of economic cycle theory from the broader realm of historical materialism, since the exploitation of new resources, foreign expansion, and even the outcomes of class struggles are causal factors integral to the cyclical theory itself. These aspects of social reality are thus also expressions of the capital-accumulation process.

Nevertheless, there is no cyclical theory actuated by this relationship, for although the pattern of changes in strictly-defined economic magnitudes is well established, the other aspects of social reality are not subject to such a rigid pattern. It is doubtful that innovations cluster in either the expansion or slump phase of the cycle, as it is that either phase shows a pattern in regard to real wages and so forth. Nor is there any strict rule regarding the growth of world trade, in which is expressed, among other things, the foreign expansion of rival power centers.

Technological innovation is certainly not socially neutral, since its application is governed by the logic of profitability. Likewise, innovation is a permanent process, since it results from a fundamental law of the capitalist process, competition among independent masses of capital. When major innovations break through to wide application they may unleash a process of long-range expansion, but not necessarily. For example, although railroad-building or the revolutionizing of urban areas by the automobile involved massive investments in heavy industry, which transformed industrial geography, there is no certainty that the current wave of innovations based on computerization will have a similar effect. This contemporary technological revolution provides no solution to the problem of surplus-absorption, which largely explains the leakage of so much of property incomes into financial speculation. In slump periods, innovation proceeds through sharpened competition, forcing firms to lower their costs of production. This is why the slump phases of the apparent cycle are also marked by a positive rate of growth of overall output, even though that rate is less than the growth rate obtained in expansion phases.

Social struggles have had indeterminable economic consequences. This is due in part to their variable placement in terms of cyclical phases, as well as to more fundamental determining factors, such as the ongoing struggles of wage earners to secure a greater share of the social product and the alliances with other social classes, such as the peasantry, formed by big capital in response to the socialist challenge. This renders illusory any attempt to form a theory of the long cycle and thus level historical materialism down into a simplistic economic determinism. As to the effects of the contest among competitive capitalist centers and of their failures and successes in foreign expansionary ventures, these are likewise irreducible to any sort of cyclical mechanism.

Each of the last three long slumps, accordingly, has its own specific nature in many respects.

The massive depression toward the close of the nineteenth century, intensifying competitive pressures, sped up the process of concentration and centralization of capital until the capitalist system was qualitatively transformed: the competitive industrial capitalism that prevailed from 1800 to 1880 gave way to oligopolistic (shared monopoly) capitalism. These oligopolies were still groups organized on an essentially national basis, despite the expansion of their activities abroad and the occasional interpenetration and cosmopolitanism of their strategies. At that time their competition sharpened the rivalry among national states, putting an end to the previously dominant position of Great Britain. This period is that in which the world was divided up among rival imperialist powers. The specific character of this new oligopolistic capitalism was assayed by Hilferding (who emphasized the interpenetration of financial and industrial capital so characteristic of German capitalism), Hobson (who observed the bank-centered nature of British capital and its cosmopolitan strategy of international expansion), and Lenin (who drew the political conclusion that the aggravation of inter-imperialist rivalries was the preliminary condition for a world socialist revolution). Although economic stagnation was the rule only for the older capitalist countries, with industrial growth speeding up elsewhere, especially in Germany and the United States, the slump was generally accompanied by a change from privately held to publicly held forms of firm ownership, through which financial capital established dominance over industrial capital—in Marx's terms, the dominance of the direct process M-M' (interest) over the production process M-C-M' (profit).

Inter-imperialist rivalry obviously constituted the most important feature of the 1914-1945 phase ("The Thirty Years War of the British Succession" between Germany and the United States), marked as it was by two world wars and the Great Depression of the 1930s. Neither the short expansion phase (1896-1913) that preceded the First World War nor the brief, dubious, boom of the 1920s allowed a new market-capitalized oligopolistic mode of capital accumulation to become stabilized. The stock market merely enriched some at the expense of others, since only the general expansion of production could offer a way out of this zero-sum game. This usurer-rentier capitalism (as Bukharin and Lenin called it) widened inequality in income distribution, both internally and internationally, and thus strengthened the prevailing stagnation and international rivalry. The system also remained governed by competition, exerting downward pressure on wages. These were the mechanisms of the deflationary spiral that Keynes analyzed toward the close of the period, thus providing the intellectual foundation for the expansionary policies of the next, postwar period.

Our current long slump—which began with the end of the 1960s—followed an expansion that, from immediately after the Second World War, was based on three factors arising from the defeat of fascism: (a) historic capital-labor compromise maintained,

in the developed capitalist countries, by Keynesian national policies that put a new form of governance over capital accumulation
in place of the wage-depressing competitive regime; (b) the "Soviet" system, called an attempt to build socialism, although it really
was an attempt to build "capitalism without capitalists," which
nevertheless set itself up as a challenge to capitalism and so
stimulated it; and (c) the attempts at national-capitalist development in the peripheral countries, which were made possible by the
victories of national liberation movements.

At the origin of our current slump is the progressive exhaustion
of these three social models, which followed from the fact, among
others, that their very successes deepened global interdependence.
This slump thus unfolds in an environment of deepened globalization, the more so since the Soviet alternative has collapsed and
the national-capitalist project in the third world could not resist
the offensive of the dominant capitalisms which aimed at reducing
the bourgeoisies of the peripheral continents to their former status
as dependent intermediaries.

While oligopolies established during the 1873-1896 slump had
to be, by and large, instruments of state policy, globalization in the
current period has given them broad autonomy. Firms now develop their own strategies without regard to "national interests"
and put pressure on states to render them instruments of corporate
policy. Rivalries among nation-states, despite the spur given them
by the decline of the postwar U.S. hegemony, are now worked out
under conditions completely different from those that marked the
period of inter-imperialist conflicts.

The current slump, like all others, is expressed through surplus
capital unable to find sufficiently profitable outlets in the expansion of productive capacity. Capitalist management of the slump
has therefore aimed at providing alternative profitable outlets in

the financial arena, and by that very fact has made the preservation of capital values its main priority, even when this is detrimental to economic growth. This new hegemony of the capital markets has acted through a variety of means, notably floating exchange rates, high interest rates, privatization of formerly state-owned enterprises, huge deficits in the U.S. balance of payments, and policies by international financial institutions forcing third world countries to put service of their foreign debt above all other considerations. As usual, such policies confine the world economy to a stagnant, vicious circle out of which they offer no escape. In fact, this stubborn stagnation affects only that half of the world—the United States, Europe, and Japan with their Latin American, African, and Middle Eastern dependencies—which is forced to undergo the measures adopted by the capital markets to manage the slump. East Asia (especially China), followed by Southeast Asia and, to some degree, India, have in contrast experienced a speeding up of their economic growth and to that extent they have escaped the impact of the slump.

IV

The history of really existing capitalism is marked, in contrast to the stability of prior systems, by a continuous succession of slumps, some short, some long, some shallow, some deep. But the inherent instability of capitalism is also its strength: during the expansion phases between the slumps it has fostered an extraordinary expansion of productive forces, incomparably greater than the slow growth prevailing in previous epochs. Despite the enormous destructive impacts of the exponential but irregular growth that has distinguished it, capitalism has transformed the conditions of human existence in a remarkably short historical span. Nevertheless, precisely because its growth is exponential (like cancer, sustained exponential growth can lead only to death) that growth cannot be sustained indefinitely. Capitalism is fated to be surpassed and, without doubt, it will show up in history as a short transition period during which the accumulation of productive forces will have created the material and human conditions for a better form of mastery over nature and social development.

To go beyond capitalism, will we necessarily have to go through a crisis that can be called systemic, general, or fundamental? Critical social thought—that type of thought characteristic of utopian, reformist, and Marxist socialist movements—has taken a special interest in this question, based as it is on the distinction between this sort of crisis *of* the system and the crises *within* the system.

Marx expected that the law of capital accumulation governing the capitalist system would quickly extend its sway over the whole world, homogenizing social conditions, and by that very fact establish the objective conditions for a worldwide socialist revolution. Because he overestimated the revolutionary role of the bourgeoisie, Marx saw worldwide expansion of productive forces as equivalent to a worldwide spread of the capitalist mode of production. But the law of value characteristic of this mode of production requires that markets become integrated in all their dimensions (markets for capital, for commodities, and for labor power). On the scale of the world capitalist system such integrating tendencies have prevailed for the first two dimensions but not at all for the third. Because it is based on this truncated nature of the world market, the law of value in its globalized form is subservient to the polarization between central and peripheral economies, which polarization is inherent in capitalism as it has developed historically and cannot be overcome within a capitalist framework. Because of this essential characteristic of the capitalist system, the theoretical and practical questions related to going beyond capitalism need to be posed in different terms than they were in the various post-Marx theories of the transition to socialism.

Lenin had been convinced by the coinciding formation of oligopolies and the calamitous aggravation of inter-imperialist rivalries that "imperialism was the highest stage of capitalism," in the sense that the workers of all countries would react to the imperialist war by a revolution which, even though it might begin in the "weakest link" of the system, would become general throughout the system. This revolution did indeed take place in Russia. But instead of extending itself westward, it was shifted toward other peripheral countries—either in a radical form (China) or in the diminished form of national liberation movements—thus revealing the decisive nature of the polarization between central and peripheral countries produced by the capitalist system.

Stalin, in his turn, theorized about the unforeseen course of history with a thesis whose formula consisted of a general crisis of capitalism, the building of "socialism in a single country," and competition between the two systems. The thesis seemed to receive confirmation from both the long interwar depression and the extension of "socialist" systems into Eastern Europe and Asia. But it covered over the nature of the so-called socialist project, whose true objective was to build a "capitalism without capitalists," which finally changed, as it had to, into a capitalism *with* capitalists.

Displaying its remarkable and characteristic flexibility, capitalism accordingly overcame its "general crisis," and after the Second World War, stimulated by its competition with the East and taking advantage of growth in those peripheral countries that regained their independence, it commenced a new stage of prodigious expansion. Nevertheless, despite this success—amplified by the collapse of the Soviet alternative—the brief postwar boom has, for the past quarter century, become bogged down in a new, prolonged slump. Is the dominance of the financial markets, which is the distinguishing characteristic of this slump, an insurmountable barrier to the materialization of a new boom phase? Can the marginalization and impoverishment accompanying the depression—this time extending over whole continents (notably Africa)—be borne indefinitely? Is the contrast between, on the one hand, the depression of the West and the peripheral countries that it dominates through intermediaries and, on the other, the East Asian industrialization, the commencement of a lessening of that colossal polarization? Or is it leading to new forms of polarization based on the five new monopolies—over technologies, financial systems, worldwide access to natural resources, media and information systems, and weapons of mass destruction—held by the imperialist centers? Will a new system of capital accumulation that is able to overcome the risk of planet-wide ecological devastation be put in place in time? Such, today, are the big questions posed by the crisis of the system. Will the flexibility of capitalism prevail over its ideological and institutional limitations? Will it in turn open unforeseen ways to go beyond its social regime? Or will those blockages divert us to a final catastrophe? Will yet another new wave of revolutions and creative adaptations provide a transition to a new form of globalization that can hardly be envisaged under current conditions?

2

Unity and Changes in the Ideology of Political Economy

As with all social sciences, the history of economic theory has not proceeded along a course like that taken by the natural sciences. In the natural sciences new theories—fuller, more complex, more accurate—ultimately take the place of formerly dominant theories, which are then completely abandoned. Of course, this development is shaped by conflicts among schools of thought, and sometimes the victory of a theory is but temporary. Nevertheless, as Kuhn has shown so well, the deepening of knowledge always ends up with the imposition of a new paradigm. The concept of science, closely linked to this progression, here takes on its full meaning.

Things stand quite differently in regard to knowledge of social reality, where schools of thought constantly oppose each other without ever attaining a definitive predominance. Such schools are defined by different—and sometimes diametrically opposed—conceptions of the real nature of their common object of analysis: society. And these oppositions transgress reality; they outlive all the changes in social reality itself. Of course, the best analysts in each of these schools are well aware of these changes and sharpen their observations and analytic techniques to take account of the new questions posed, but even so they always remain within the bounds of their own chosen paradigm.

This difference, then, characterizes the different status of scientific analysis in the fields of nature and society: it reminds us that human beings, as individuals and as social actors, make their own history, while they can merely observe the history of the natural world. In regard to society, science (in the sense of a respect for facts) and ideology (in the sense of a point of view justifying social conservatism or social transformation) are inseparable. And that is why I prefer to speak of "social thought" (without implying any evasion of the requirements of scientific method) rather than of "social science."

Concerning the modern history of capitalism, we have had for the last two centuries two opposing lines of argument, and never will the partisans of one of them succeed in convincing those of the other. On one side is the conservative line of discourse, which justifies the capitalist social order, and on the other is that of socialism with its radical critique of that order. This is not to say that they dispute in a circle, tirelessly repeating the same arguments. For the capitalism about which they argue is itself in constant evolution, and at each of its phases the requirements for its further development call for different policies. The most interesting point of view within the conservative (pro-capitalist) current is that which succeeds in justifying these necessary policies and in showing the most effective means for their implementation. On the other side of the tracks, the social problems created by this development are themselves changed, some lessening or vanishing, others newly arising or becoming intensified; the most effective point of view within the radically critical current is that which best sizes up the new challenges.

Social thought, accordingly, is always closely linked to the question of social power, either by justifying a given established system of power or by challenging it by proposing a different one. Among the entirety of conceptions making up bourgeois thought, that one which responds best to the demands posed by the particular phase of capitalist development under consideration easily wins its place of intellectual dominance; it becomes the "single thought" of the moment. In contrast, ideological pluralism tends to be the rule to the extent that the intellectual critique of capitalism relates only oppositionally to established power. Nevertheless, precisely because there was, from 1917 to 1990, a really existing system of established power claiming the status of socialist alternative, a dominant social ideology inextricably linked to the Soviet power structure was also imposed within the socialist ranks. An alternative "single thought," expressed in language inspired by vulgar Marxism, coexisted with the succeeding forms of capitalist single thought—liberal nationalist, Keynesian, neoliberal globalist—that have held the stage during this period. With the collapse of the Soviet alternative, the "single thought" of "really existing socialism" vanished. Into its place have swarmed radical critiques of a diverse scope. These have not yet crystallized into coherent alternative projects, formulated as renewed systems of critical thought that would be sufficiently powerful to give effective answers to the challenges of the contemporary world. The bourgeois single thought of the moment thus holds universal sway, without the need to share that influence as it did during the period of ideological dualism. However, this is not a new situation: dominant bourgeois thought, in the forms appropriate to the requirements of the 1800-1914 expansion of capitalism, was also, by and large, the universal single thought for each successive stage of that expansion.

Thus the dominant line of thought of capitalism is displayed as a succession of forms which, beyond the diversity of their modalities of expression, remain organized around an unchanging core of basic conceptions and methods. To point out the permanence of this hard core and to identify the real scope of the successive and varied modalities of capitalist discourse is to understand both what is permanent in capitalism and what is specific to each phase in its blossoming. Thus we can see the place of each successive "single thought" in the history of capitalist society.

The characteristic ideology of capitalism has always been economic determinist. This gives a dominant position to the subject matter of what has become economic theory. Yet this (and the autonomy that economic theory derives from it) does not fully comprise it. For it is also the product of a social and political philosophy that underlies the concept of individual freedom and defines the limits within which modern political democracy is practiced. The characteristics and contradictions of conventional economic theory flow from this ambiguous position in the ideological rhetoric of capitalism. Indeed, this economic theory is strung out between two extreme positions. At one pole its practitioners seek to construct a "pure economics" (according to their own terminology) that follows only its own self-contained set of laws, free from such dimensions of social reality as the organization of societies as nations, political practice, and state intervention. This perpetual tendency in conventional economic theory thus seeks to formulate a rigorous theory (by its own specific criteria) of how a general equilibrium is produced through the self-regulating nature of the market. But at its other pole these economists choose deliberately to put themselves at the service of the really existing power structure, in order to suggest effective actions to regulate the market and to enhance their nation's position in the world system. However, these really existing power structures are not at all identical to each other irrespective of space and time. To say that they all maintain the power of the bourgeoisie is quite insufficient, even though the statement is not false. For this power is imposed through hegemonic social coalitions specific to particular countries and historical periods, a fact which requires state policies that maintain the compromises among social classes that define such coalitions. Economic theory is then formulated in terms suited to these objectives, and stays far away from the abstract preoccupations of pure economics.

The single thought is generally expressed through successive formulations of this second type, with "pure economics" relegated to the status of academic palaver without any bearing on real life. The fact remains that at certain exceptional times—and the grounds for these exceptions demand explanation—the single thought comes close to the propositions of pure economics or even merges into them. We are currently in one of those periods.

I will not at this point hark back to the reasons why the capitalist worldview is naturally economic determinist. This characteristic follows from an objective requirement, without which capitalism cannot function: the inversion of the relation between politics and economics characteristic of precapitalist social systems so that politics becomes subordinate to economics. This objective requirement creates the space for the establishment of an "economic science" whose laws govern the reproduction process of capitalist society which really appears—and it is in this that it breaks with its past—to be determined by those laws. It is this reversal of the relationship between politics and economics that of necessity demands the formulation of "pure economic theory."

Nor will I dwell long on the history of this theory's establishment. It took place just as soon as capitalism—with the

Industrial Revolution at the start of the nineteenth century—took on its completed form. It was at first expressed in a clumsy form that (as in Bastiat) represented little more than unconditional praise for the "market"—a form that Marx for this very reason rightly termed vulgar economics. Later, mathematical techniques would be used (as in Walras) to express the interdependence of markets in a theory of general equilibrium.

To show that capitalism can function (that it does function is a matter of fact) is not the sole concern of this theory, which remains the inescapable hard core of capitalist rhetoric. It is equally necessary to prove that this rational functioning answers to the expectations of individuals and peoples, which in turn makes capitalism not only legitimate but even "eternal." It represents "the end of history." Such a proof necessarily requires re-establishment of the linkage between economic theory and social and political philosophy. Economic discourse would thus be enriched to become the general discourse of capitalism, transcending the economic basis of its argument.

The relationship linking conventional economic theory to its underlying social philosophy spreads over numerous subjects. I will here deal with two of them, the theory of value and the concept of individual freedom.

The choice to base the concept of value on social labor or on individual and subjective estimation of utility is itself the result of the opposition between two concepts of social reality. The second of these choices, which became crystallized into a theory of pure economics only at a late stage, after (and in response to) Marx, defines society as a collection of individuals, nothing more. It seems to me that, despite being formulated in ever more sophisticated ways, the attempt to formulate on this basis the theorems that would allow proof both that the system functions and reproduces itself (general equilibrium) and that it simultaneously is the best possible (by maximizing individual gratifications), fails to reach its objective. But that is not what concerns us here. In contrast, the first choice, because it is based on measurable quantities, has fed into a succession of positivist depictions of capitalist reality, from Walrasian general equilibrium which has been taken up again and reformulated by Maurice Allais (in an attempt to synthesize the positive interdependence of markets with subjective valuation) to the purely positivist system of Piero Sraffa.

The positivist mentality inspiring the evolution of this current within conventional economic theory allows for the possibility of communication between the economic discourse of capitalism and that of its critics, or at least, as we will see further on, with one possible line of critical thought.

No less important is the relationship between the theory of pure economics, in all its variants, and the bourgeois philosophy of individual freedom. We here have a philosophy that was produced by the bourgeoisie both as an act of self-affirmation in the face of the ancien régime and as the basis of its own social and economic system. This system is of course not summed up by the single notion of individual freedom, although it holds a decisive position in economic theory. *Homo oeconomicus* is a free individual who chooses whether to sell his labor or refrain from work, whether to innovate or to conform, whether to buy or to sell. The exercise of such freedom requires that society be organized on the basis of generalized markets—for labor, for products, for business firms.

This principle has as a logical consequence that social reality should produce all the conditions, and only the conditions, for the exercise of this freedom—in other words, this logic rejects as irrational any association of these individuals into communities (for example, into nations), rejects the historically constituted state, and even, as we will see, rejects private property. Under these conditions all the individuals comprising the population of the planet can meet in the marketplace to negotiate their mutual relationships on terms of perfect equality, since none of them would hold a privileged position through ownership of even the smallest capital. A state/administration/bank positioned above these individuals, on a world scale of course, would be charged with managing this generalized marketplace. Would-be entrepreneurs would propose their projects for its judgment. The state/bank would lend capital to those favored by its judgment. Other individuals would negotiate the sale of their labor to these entrepreneurs, and all products would be bought and sold by fully informed participants on open markets. This logic, when pushed to an extreme, frightens defenders of capitalism, and for this reason it is rarely expressed (although Walras, like his successor Allais, did begin to give it consideration). In contrast, some social thinkers critical of capitalism found themselves comfortable with this logic. They accordingly have imagined a market that would be planned in this way so as to be perfect, unlike that of really existing capitalism—and, what is more, would be perfectly equitable because it would be based on the equality of all citizens (of a single country or of the world). This sort of socialism, of which Barone was a theoretical precursor, looks very much like capitalism—a capitalism without (private) capitalists or, more exactly, without hereditary owners of capital. But it belongs within that line of critical thought which does not call into question capitalism's inherent economic determinism (the alienated form of economic life inseparable from the market). This tendency likewise accepts the arguments of the positivist general-equilibrium analysis as expressed in labor-value terms. In this way it provided elements for the conception of what was to become socialist economic planning. We will return to this point later.

The bourgeois conception of individual freedom as accepted by pure economics (whether capitalist or socialist) is that of right-wing anarchism—hostile to the state, to organizations (including trade unions), and, in principle, to monopolies. It thus has wide appeal among small businessmen and, as is well known, was a component in the attraction of the 1920s fascist and protofascist movements for these confused sections of the middle class. But it can also turn into statism, as was the case for all historic forms of fascism. These waverings stem from the fact that "pure economics" (and the "market-governed society" inspired by it) is a utopia. It is, in reality, dependent on hypotheses that exclude all those aspects of really existing capitalism that trouble its rhetoric, such as states, nations, social classes, and global interdependencies, just as it abstracts from the exclusive ownership of the means of production by a minority, from the forms of real competition (like oligopolies), and from the rules limiting access to the use of natural resources. But reality, excluded from this ideological discourse, gets its own back and, in the end, prevails.

Behind the abstract discourse on pure market economics lurks a real, and very different, model of the market. This model, to begin with, is dualistic: integrated in its three dimensions (markets for products, labor, and capital) at the national level, but curtailed and reduced to only two of these three (markets for products and capital, but not for labor) at the global level. Accordingly, this duality manifests as conflict among nations within the global system and so compels the rhetoric of right-wing anarchism to merge into that of nationalism. More-over, the economic determinist alienation at the source of the capitalist utopia we are discussing likewise leads to treating natural resources as mere objects of market trading, with all the consequences that follow from this reduction.

Because pure capitalism does not exist, and because really existing capitalism is not an approximation of it but an altogether different sort of thing, the theorems characteristic of pure economics are meaningless and its behavioral rules and propositions have no application. So our ideologues have to accept that contesting states and nations exist, that competition is oligopolistic, that the distribution of property determines the distribution of income, and so forth. To hold onto the rhetoric of pure economics, they extend it with proposals for concrete economic policies that allegedly meet the criteria for a "second best" optimization, even though they are nothing of the sort. These proposals quite simply express the demands of politicians at the service of interests whose very existence pure economics denies in principle: the nation, the ruling classes, or some ruling-class faction, depending on the balance of social power characterizing one or another stage in the history of capitalism.

It must thus be understood that the bourgeois single thought generally does not take on the extreme, virtually absurd, forms of the capitalist utopia. This single thought is expressed most frequently, and most forcefully, in realistic forms appropriate to concrete situations. It brings together the market, the state, and the nation to serve the social compromises needed for the functioning of coalitions among dominant class interests.

I am not going to put forward here a history of the successive forms of the capitalist single thought. I will merely consider a few of its broad features, relevant to the modern period.

From the latter part of the nineteenth century, from about 1880—when monopoly capitalism became established in the sense given that term by Hobson, Hilferding, and Lenin—to

1945, the capitalist single thought could well be called "monopolistic nationalist liberalism." "Liberalism" here signifies a double
affirmation: affirmation on the one hand of the predominant role
of markets (oligopolistic markets, to be sure) in a self-regulating
economy within the structure of appropriate public policies applied during this period, and on the other hand, of bourgeois-
democratic political practices. Nationalism was a regulating fact
within this liberal model able to legitimize the public policies
underlying competition within the global system. Those policies
hinged on local hegemonic coalitions (alliances with middle-class
and aristocratic strata) that backed up the dominant power of
capitalist monopolies and kept the industrial working class in
political isolation. Notable examples were the British and German
regulatory systems, based on protection of aristocratic privilege
and of Junker landholdings, and the French system, based on
support to peasant farming and family-scale small business. Likewise, these alliances were generally rounded out and reinforced
through colonial privileges. Electoral democracy, based on these
alliances, allowed ongoing flexible adjustment of the terms for
their maintenance. This model, without being statist, was nevertheless at the opposite pole from the anti-state right-wing anarchist
approach. The state was needed for management of the hegemonic
coalition by organizing and regulating markets appropriately (for
example, by subsidizing agriculture) and for directing its international competitive strategy (through protective tariffs and monetary regulation). Its active intervention in this sense was considered
perfectly legitimate, even necessary. A whole world separated the
single thought of that epoch from the utopia of pure capitalism.
The latter's votaries could survive only by retreating into the
academic world, where as always they went on accusing history of

being wrong because it was unfolding without regard to the logic of pure economics. By that very fact they had no influence at all.

The monopolistic nationalist liberal single thought fell into crisis when the system it underlay entered into the crisis that began in 1914, as economic competition turned into world war. I regard its fascist deviation of the interwar period as within this same structure. Fascism abandoned the politically democratic aspect of the system, but renounced neither nationalism (which, on the contrary, it aggravated) nor the internal social compromises that bolstered the power of the monopolies. Fascist thought was thus a component, even though a sick one, of the ruling single thought of this long phase in the history of capitalism.

During this period, the liberal single thought was not based on an anarchist conception of individual freedom. To the contrary, freedom was supposed to need laws and a law-based state in order to flourish properly. Nevertheless, the notion of democracy remained limited: the rights of the individual were those guaranteeing formal juridical equality, freedom of expression, and, up to a certain point, freedom of association. But nothing more: still embryonic were the rights that later would show up (in the counter-model of really existing socialism after 1917 as well as in the later stage of capitalism after 1945) as special social rights required to give real effect to the general rights.

The liberal nationalist single thought entered into crisis when the claim of economic theory to maintain a harmoniously working society was contradicted by reality. This economic theory, which was made into a comprehensive and integrated whole (of which Alfred Marshall undoubtedly gave the fullest account) at exactly this moment in history, was "a rhetoric of universal harmonies." In substance, it claimed to prove that markets (structured through adequate public policies) were self-regulating (in the sense that their workings correct for all imbalances between supply and demand). But it was not, in this regard, limited to an abstract and general proof. It applied to all the dimensions of economic reality. For example, it presented a theory of the business cycle that filled out, by applying it concretely, the general theory of the self-regulating ability of the market. The parallel to this was a theory of fluctuations in the balance of payments that provided for automatic maintenance of equilibrium at the global level. The picture was completed by a theory of monetary management as determined by the requirement of maintaining the regulatory power of the market mechanisms.

But starting exactly in 1914, all of these promises of harmony became inoperative. Nevertheless, throughout the interwar years this single thought continued to prevail and its prescriptions, such as national protectionism, competing strong currencies, and cuts in wages and government spending in response to recession, went on being imposed. Was this a case of simple mental inertia? The answer to this question is not to be sought in the debates over economic theories but is to be found at the level of the real balance of social forces underlying the policies prevailing during this period. Until the New Deal in the United States and the Popular Front in France, the working class remained weak and isolated. Under those conditions, why indeed should capital have made any concessions to it? In the debate over economic ideas, it was specifically Keynes who indicted the single thought of the interwar period, proving that it prompted the economic policies that worsened the slump. Nevertheless, this critique had no impact on policy. It took the Second World War, which upset the balance of social forces in favor of the working classes and oppressed peoples, for its message to be understood and to become central to the new version of the single thought.

This explains why a new single thought, starting in 1945, took the place of liberal nationalism and prevailed on the world scene until 1980. Indeed, the Second World War, through the defeat of fascism, changed the relationship of forces in favor of the working classes in the developed countries of the West (these classes gained a legitimacy and status that they had never theretofore possessed), of the colonial peoples who freed themselves, and of the countries of "really existing socialism" (which I would rather call Sovietism). This new relationship is behind the threefold construction of welfare states based on national Keynesian policies, of development states in the Third World, and of planned state socialism. I would therefore describe the single thought of the 1945-1980 period as "social and national," operating within the framework of a controlled globalization.

Karl Polanyi was the first to understand the nature and bearing of the crystallization of this new thought, which was to become the single thought of the postwar period. I will not dwell here on his critique of the 1880-1945 liberalism that was responsible for the catastrophe. In a frontal attack on the capitalist utopia he showed that labor, nature, and money could be treated as commodities only at the cost of the alienation and degradation of human beings, the pitiless destruction of the planet's resources, and the subversion of the government-money relationship to the profit of financial speculators. These three basic features of liberalism's irrationality were to surface again after 1980.

The dominant single thought of the 1945-1980 years was thus built, at least in part, on the critique of liberalism. That is why I described it as "social and national," intentionally omitting the word "liberal" in order to underline this fact. The new single thought, often simplistically called "Keynesian," remained, of course, a capitalist way of thinking. That is why it did not make a radical break with the basic dogmas of liberalism, but merely rearranged them incompletely. Labor was still treated as a commodity, but the severity of its treatment was mitigated through the three principles of collective bargaining, social insurance, and wage increases proportional to productivity increases. Contrariwise, natural resources remained the object of systematic and aggravated wastage, which is the inescapable consequence of the absurd "discounting of the future" characteristic of "rational" short-run economic calculation (whereas what we need is the exact contrary—to give greater value to the future). Money, on the other hand, was thereafter subject to political control at both governmental and global levels. (The purpose of Bretton Woods was to maintain stable exchange rates.)

The two adjectives "social" (not socialist) and "national" express well the essential political objectives operative during this period and, consequently, the methods employed for those purposes. It was held that solidarity—which was expressed in a remarkable stability of income distribution, in full employment, and in continual increases in social expenditures—needed to be maintained on the national level through policies of systematic state intervention (described as "Keynesian" or, rather, "neo-Keynesian" policies). Reformulation of these policies in terms of (Fordist or welfarist) "regulation" allowed specification of the grounds for the validity and effectiveness of state intervention as thus conceived. Nevertheless, this nationalism, indubitable, never amounted to all-out nationalism. For it was circumscribed within a general climate of regionalization (as the building of "Europe" attests) and of an accepted, even desired, but controlled globalization through such efforts as the Marshall Plan, the expansion of multinational corporations, UNCTAD, GATT, and the organization of collective North-South discussions within the UN framework.

The basic aims of these welfare state practices were analogous to those of modernization and industrialization for the newly independent countries of the third world, which I call the Bandung project for Asia and Africa with its parallel, *desarrollismo* (developmentalism) in Latin America. We can thus characterize this single thought as dominant on the global scale, excluding only the zone of Sovietism. For the third world countries, an equally important objective was to overcome their backwardness through effective and controlled entry into a world system undergoing sustained growth.

Thus, the single thought of the 1945-1980 phase was not merely an "economic theory" (that of Keynesianism and the macroeconomic management flowing from it) but was likewise the expression of a true corporate project which, though capitalist, was also "social." And within this framework, it must be understood, substantial progress was realized in regard to specific social rights that gave concrete expression to general rights. The right to work and the rights of workers; the rights to education, health, and welfare assistance; the establishment of pension and retirement funds; and the readjustment of pay scales in favor of working women—all these were always presented as the very objectives of economic growth and development. Of course, the actual achievements in these domains were uneven and generally dependent on the strength of progressive social movements.

Four decades after the end of the Second World War this model had used up its potential for expansion. It is this evolution, with its parallel in the exhaustion of the Sovietist countermodel, that lies at the origin of the overall crisis of the system which began in 1980 and accelerated throughout the next decade to end in 1990 with the generalized collapse of the three component subsystems of the prior phase (the welfare state, the Bandung project, and the

Sovietist system). It was this crisis, unfolding on the level of reality, that caused the collapse of the "social and national" single thought which had been operative in the framework of the "controlled globalization" of the postwar phase. This collapse was obviously not the result of debates about "economic theory" in which "young" neoliberals (pupils of Von Hayek, Chicago-school monetarists, etc.) were opposed by "socialist dinosaurs," as is sometimes suggested by the polemicists who currently hold the stage.

The new period, which opened with the collapse of the prior phase's real-growth models, has itself not yet had enough time to become stabilized. That is why I have analyzed it in terms of "chaos" rather than a new national or global order, and why I have analyzed its practices in terms of "crisis management" and not of a new growth model.

This observation informs the description I have here put forward of the new crisis-impelled single thought. This thought, which is put forward as "globalized neoliberalism," can be more precisely characterized as a social neoliberalism, operative within globalization gone wild. By that very fact, it is impracticable, incapable of any sort of actual or full realization. Its constituent dogmas (privatization, free trade, flexible exchange rates, cuts in public spending, deregulation) are too well known to need discussion here. They cannot last because they shut capitalism into a fatal stagnation, shutting all the doors that might let it overcome the slump and begin a new growth period. I have given elsewhere the grounds for this judgment, which I share with Paul Sweezy and Harry Magdoff, namely that the single-minded pursuit of profit maximization, even were it not to clash with anti-system forces representing the aspirations of workers and oppressed peoples, would inescapably involve a structural disequilibrium in which supply exceeded demand. In other words, contrary to the pseudotheoretical dogma of capitalist utopia (the theory of pure economics), markets are not self regulating. To work, they need government regulation.

The hard choices imposed by the new single thought do not stem from some intellectual waywardness that allowed their advocates to win a theoretical debate. They are the product of a new relationship of forces, extremely favorable to capital, since the working classes and the peripheral nations have steadily lost the positions of strength they had held at the moment when fascism was defeated. The development models on which they based themselves having become worn out, the popular forces have not yet had time to regroup around new social projects that would be adequate, possible, and acceptable to them. This imbalance is at the origin of the sway of speculative capital markets, an analysis of which I have put forward elsewhere.

Though these hard choices are generally dominant in rhetorical discourse, the reality is that they are applied in a way that at times flagrantly contradicts the dogmas from which they stem. The vaunted globalization remains curtailed to the detriment of labor markets and, to an ever-increasing extent, by strengthened restrictions against immigration; rhetoric about the virtue of competition barely hides how in practice monopolies are systematically defended (as is visible in the dealings of the new World Trade Organization, or WTO); and insistence on discounting the future reduces to zero the significance of environmentalist discourse. Finally, belying their affirmation of internationalist principles, the Great Powers (conspicuously the United States) continually apply raw power in all domains, whether military (the Persian Gulf War) or economic (the "Super 301" clause in the U.S. foreign trade law).

Of course, the new single thought and the policies following from it are directed at systematically dismantling the specific rights that had been achieved by the workers and lower classes. Given this, all its discourse about democracy is exposed as empty rhetoric, unrelated to reality. In practice, democracy based on an organized citizenry is being replaced by the right-wing anarchist utopia. Reality then lashes back through the emergence of communal, ethnic, and fundamentalist religious particularisms, confronting an ineffectual state and a disruptive marketplace.

The current single thought has no future. As a symptom of the crisis, it offers no solutions but is itself part of the problem.

The single thought of capitalist political economy has always been based on an imperialist world view, in accord with the development of capitalism which, by its very nature, has always been uneven and polarizing on the world scale. During the monopolistic nationalist liberal phase (from 1880 to 1945), imperialism was (or rather imperialisms were) synonymous with conflict among imperialist powers, in the Leninist sense. In contrast, the social and national postwar phase (1945 to 1980) was characterized on the one hand by the strategic convergence of national imperialisms under the discipline of a hegemonic United States, and on the other by a retreat of imperialism, which was forced to withdraw from the regions of "real socialism" (the U.S.S.R., Eastern Europe, China) and to bargain with national liberation movements over the terms under which it would maintain its position in its Asian, African, and Latin American peripheries. Now that "really existing socialism" and third world radical populism have met their ruin, imperialism is once again on the offensive. The "globalization" thesis proclaimed so arrogantly by the current ideology is nothing but a new way in which the inherently imperialist nature of the system asserts itself. In this sense, it can be said that "globalization" is a euphemism for that forbidden word, imperialism.

Of course, the permanently imperialist dimension of the capitalist political economy is never admitted. The material advantages associated with imperialism—notably the superprofits enjoyed by dominant capitalists—are always buried under the vaguest possible rhetoric about "international competition." Assertions about such age-old competition, which antedates the modern system of global capitalism, can mean everything or nothing. For this competition is governed not by purported natural laws (such as racial inequality) or pseudonatural laws (such as the uniqueness of cultures, or the laws of the market as alleged by economic theory), but by the strategic options of nations and peoples within the logical framework specific to each successive historical system.

Can we hope to see the reconstitution of a coherent and effective anticapitalist discourse, in confrontation with the capitalist rhetoric whose major features, expressed simultaneously in its singular character and its successive adaptations, I have outlined? I will not here try to answer this question, which goes beyond our topic. I will merely say that anticapitalist discourse is truly radical only when it deals with the basic and permanent features of capitalism, and in the first instance with the alienated nature of economic behavior. That, in my opinion, was the meaning of Marx's project.

Yet there have been partially anticapitalist discourses developed during the real history of the last two centuries, which, despite their limits, have proven effective in some ways. Without them, neither Western social democracy, nor Eastern state socialism, nor the Southern project of national liberation could have existed. These anticapitalist discourses were able to impose on the dominant sectors of capital those historic compromises which forced it to adapt to the popular and working-class demands expressed in the above-mentioned three instances. The Sovietist alternative model stemmed from this sort of unradical critique of capitalism, with the result that in reality it led to "capitalism without capitalists." But here also, as always, that evolution was not the result of a special theoretical outlook (not even though it could be considered a "deviation" from Marxist proposals) but was the result of real challenges confronting the societies at issue and real relationships of social forces marking them. As always, the theory was produced by reality, not the other way around.

3

Is Social History Marked by Overdetermination or Underdetermination?

Louis Althusser's concept of overdetermination follows directly from his structuralist concept of social systems. He suggests, at least implicitly if not explicitly, that the determining factors at work alongside each other in various instances of social reality are in fact convergent, because they all contribute simultaneously to the reproduction of the system, to its adaptation to what is required for its evolution, and to the crisis that will eventually propel society beyond it. The economic determinants, and those that govern politics, ideology, and culture, all work in the same direction and consequently "overdetermine" social evolution. Thus, if a transformation is economically necessary, it also is politically, ideologically, and culturally necessary—and the reciprocal is also the case. If one accepts that the economic factor is, in the last analysis, decisive, the notion of overdetermination can easily lead to an economic determinist reading of history, in which the other factors adapt themselves to the requirements of the economic one.

This is certainly a possible interpretation of Marxism, and I would not be so presumptuous as to deny this reading by, for example, calling it "deviationist" or, even worse, "heretical." But it is not my interpretation of Marxism, for at least two reasons.

The first reason is that I do not think it right to pose the question of the relationships among various determining influences as though similar terms apply to all the stages of history. I have often said and repeated that economics as an autonomous factor is specific to capitalism, while in former, tributary, systems it is subordinate to politics. This observation is perhaps not incompatible with the Althusserian theory, and some of his pupils have integrated it into the system of their master by suggesting a distinction between decisiveness in the last analysis and dominance. I consider this a useful proposition, and I myself have adopted it precisely to formulate the distinguishing difference between tributary systems (in which politics is dominant) and capitalism (in which economics is dominant). All that is certainly quite familiar to those who have read my writings on this subject. I will not dwell on it.

The second reason is, on the contrary, totally incompatible with Althusserian structuralism and, consequently, with his concept of overdetermination. According to my thesis, each of the determining factors is governed by its own logic, whether its status be that of last-analysis determinance (economics) or dominance (political in tributary systems, economic in capitalism, or, as I maintain, cultural in the communist future). These specific logics are autonomous, and complementarity among them does not necessarily ensue, even spontaneously. They frequently clash with each other, and it is *a priori* impossible to foresee which of them will predominate. In my opinion, Marx perfectly analyzed the economic logic of capitalism, and the accumulation of capital, as its dominant trait, that is to say, the channels through which economic logic is imposed onto political, ideological, and cultural logics. On the other hand, I have said that neither Marx nor the historical forms of Marxism have put forward comparably powerful analyses dealing with the logics of the other determining factors. Moreover I do not believe that non-Marxian theories have made any significant contribution in these regards.

The conflict among determining factors, through which each expresses its own logic, gives to history its own specific range of uncertainty, and this distinguishes it from fields governed by natural law. Neither social nor individual histories are "programmed." Freedom is defined precisely by this conflict of logics, which allows choice among different possible alternatives. Therefore, against the concept of overdetermination I advocate that of underdetermination.

Does this mean that societies are incoherent? Not at all; they always are coherent in the sense that the conflict among logics (underdetermination) always finds a solution, one among several possible solutions, through the subordination of some logics to others. Social, political, ideological, and economic struggles mold societies by forcing them to choose one type of coherence rather than another.

In contemporary discussions the autonomy of these different logics has been emphasized by various participants, most notably the autonomy of a unity (itself complex) among political, ideological, and cultural factors. Nevertheless, I do not consider that the various theses put forward on these subjects are really strong enough to carry conviction (at least not with me). They point out problems, but give no answers. This weakness is frequently expressed in sentences like "such-and-such analysis or conceptualization is economic determinist, and disregards political or cultural factors." Yes, they are disregarded, but how is one to overcome such "disregard" and demonstrate the complementary (overdetermining) or conflictual (underdetermining) relationship of the logics at issue?

It is easy for me to agree with Jean Baudrillard that value has a symbolic dimension, that the domination of power centers over the system as a whole is related to the fact that those centers are also the producers of the meanings and signs that are indispensable to everyone. But how does this production of meaning operate? What are the symbols at issue, and what is it that makes them what they are? Discourse about these subjects has remained very vague, even though here and there interesting and pregnant insights have been expressed, as was the case in its time with Freudian Marxism or, today, with the critique of patriarchy.

On the other hand I find it very difficult to accept the idea that strong cultural logics, each very different from one another, have prevailed over what Braudel calls the long run, that is to say, over a span sufficiently long enough to include within it social and economic changes important enough to be considered qualitative transformations. I have criticized this idea, which I have termed "culturalist," and which, in this moment of crisis, has the wind in its sails (on this topic see my critique of postmodernism). I have not rejected this idea on the grounds of its "anti-Marxism" (a sort of theological reasoning for which I have only contempt) but because I believe that I have shown it to be belied by history. For example, I have recognized that what people claim as their own diverse "cultural particularities" (particular to Christian "occidentals," or to the Muslim or Confucian worlds) have in reality operated in a very similar way in various tributary societies of the past. They should therefore be considered "generalities," even though taking on particular forms. I have likewise recognized that capitalism constituted a break in the cultural history of Europe, not a continuity. On these grounds I have affirmed—in contradistinction to Serge Latouche's "Westernization of the world" thesis—that the predominant culture of our modern epoch is not "Western" but is really and truly capitalist. By this I mean first of all that this culture—which can be described in terms of Promethean dynamism—was not that of medieval and Christian Europe. It is another matter altogether that Europeans, having broken with their own past, should have wished to deny that past by claiming for themselves mythical ancestors present in both their past and current history (see my explication of this matter in *Eurocentrism*). I also mean, when I choose to describe modern culture as capitalist, that the essential features of this culture are easily explained by the basic features of capitalism. Cultural dynamism is not at the origin of the dynamism of capital accumulation (though this is what Max Weber basically maintained). On the contrary, it is the dynamism of capital accumulation (which is effortlessly explained through competitive pressures on every capitalist) that carries in its wake the dynamically changing modern culture.

Also worthy of mention are other attempts, quite outside the scope of Marxist discussions, to analyze social change on the basis of an avowed irreducibility of different structural levels to any economic or other "common denominator." I refer here especially to the theses of those called postmodernists. I will put forward a critique of them in a later chapter, because these propositions seem to me to be typical in all ways of the social thought characteristic of moments of crisis like the present. Out of an almost morbid fear of falling into "past excesses" (as shown by their critique of "broad narratives" and their mistrust of conceptual thought), they calmly accept a complementary function to the ideas needed to legitimize the globalized neoliberal economics prevalent at this moment. Postmodernism, for all these reasons, has remained sterile insofar as it provides no way to account for the specific logics of those non-economic factors.

All that being the case, the charge of economic determinism against the main historic form of Marxism is valid and well established, whereas the charge that Marxism is inherently economic determinist is quite dubious. Even though neither Marx nor the Marxists have yet produced specific theories of ideology, politics, and culture comparable to their economic theory—no more than have the non-Marxists—Marx's approach calls out for just that. There is thus a noneconomic-determinist interpretation of Marxism, to which I adhere.

Social classes under capitalism (not in "all modes of production" as was stated in the Second and Third Internationals' popularizations of Marxism) are not defined solely by their relationship to the production and distribution of surplus value. As I read Marx, capitalism is based on economic alienation, in contrast to earlier forms of society based on other forms of alienation (which may be regarded as metaphysical). Alienation of labor is no less basic than its exploitation in our analysis of social classes in the modern world. To go beyond capitalism, therefore, requires not merely a "rectified apportionment of value" (which would lead only to an imaginary "capitalism without capitalists") but rather the liberation of mankind from economic alienation.

I maintain that, although historical forms of Marxism have forgotten it, Marx's critique of "economic efficiency" represents merely a particular form of rationality rather than being in itself the expression of rationality in general. Here again I refer to what I have written elsewhere, especially in regard to the so-called environmental dimensions of the question of capital accumulation.

Undoubtedly, social classes do not represent the only social realities, not even in the modern world, not even in its advanced centers. But in pointing out the existence of other forms of social solidarity—that of nations or various communities and social groupings—does one do anything more than point to the existence of other logics other than the economic one? Here again, until substantial progress has been made in the analysis of the political, ideological, and cultural logics there will be no progress in the analysis of those social solidarities, whether they complement or conflict with those stemming from the organization of society into classes.

The discussion ought to be carried beyond the identification of social classes to deal with actual and possible "class alliances" both in the metropolitan centers and in the peripheral countries of the polarized global system. I will only comment very briefly on these questions, which I have taken up in other writings.

First: In the centers, do we have social democracy or social imperialism? Even if they were social imperialist, the social compromises in the metropolitan countries (the welfare state) are not irreversible, as proven by the neoliberal efforts to dismantle them. The workers' revolt against capitalism cannot be reduced to class struggles within the framework of the capitalist mode of production, no matter how important these might be; it is, or can, also be the rejection of alienation (1968 shows this) and as such calls for going beyond the framework within which capitalism reproduces itself.

Second: Is the historical goal of bourgeois imperialism merely economic, or does it call for reflection concerning the role of nations in history? Of course I do not believe that to pose such a question is to "go outside of Marxism." It is, on the contrary, a response to what was anticipated above, the need to show how politics is linked to economics.

Third: If neoliberalism persists and achieves its goals, will the new globalization restore the commonality of the "active" and "reserve" armies of labor in central and peripheral countries, and by that very fact will it (as Giovanni Arrighi suggests) give a revolutionary role back to the working classes?

Fourth: Was the Sovietist model "statist," proving thus that a ruling class can establish its existence through politics, or was it an attempt at "capitalism without capitalists" destined, as reality has now shown, not to be overthrown by a capitalist counterrevolution but to evolve naturally into a "capitalism with capitalists"?

Fifth: Should the peripheral bourgeoisies, whose essential function is that of intermediary for world capital, still be characterized as bourgeois? Or are they merely comprador political classes?

4

Social Revolution and Cultural Revolution

Since underdetermination rather than overdetermination typifies the conflictual way in which the logics governing the various factors of social causation are interrelated, any social revolution (understanding a revolutionary change as affecting the political and economic organization of a society) must of necessity also be a cultural revolution. Or, to put it differently, in the absence of a cultural revolution (because the logic governing this social determinant has operated as an obstruction) no social revolution is possible.

The historical process through which the modern capitalist world took shape provides a good illustration of my hypothesis. Capitalism can certainly not be reduced to its economic dimension, describable as a generalized market for the products of free wage labor and for capital (by which we mean those means of production which have themselves been produced by social labor), nor yet, more basically and in conformity to the methodology of Marxism, can it be reduced to its specific production relations, which are themselves linked to an advanced level and a special structure of the productive forces. Its ideological dimensions—the uniqueness of economic alienation and, with it, the affirmation of economic activity as both autonomous and dominant over the other social determinants—likewise stand as integral elements in the concept of a capitalist mode of production, which I do not reduce to the status of an economic structure, though such treatment is frequent in Marxist popularizations. I have expressed this complex and all-embracing character of the capitalist mode of production by stating that the law of value governs not only the economic reproduction of capitalism, but all the aspects of social life under this system.

However, this analysis needs to be extended further. The modern world (as a capitalist world) is based on its own specific culture (described for that reason as "capitalist" and not as "Western"), which can be characterized by its three main components: first, individual freedom (in the bourgeois sense of the concept of freedom); second, the autonomous character of human reason, liberated from the bonds of religious faith (whereas a major concern in earlier, metaphysically alienated epochs was to reconcile faith and reason); and third, the establishment of an indissoluble link between reason and liberation, even though the latter word is conceptualized in strictly bourgeois terms (as a law-governed state, equality of individuals before the law, etc.).

The decisive moments in the crystallization of this true cultural revolution are well known: the Renaissance; then the Enlightenment, with its economic expression in mercantilism and its political expression as absolute monarchy in contrast to the earlier feudal political structures; and finally the social contract, on the basis of which new forms of government were built whose most coherent expressions were the American and, above all, the French Revolutions. This is a historical process that proceeded over the three or four centuries preceding the Industrial Revolution, after which capitalism took on its completed form.

This history certainly poses a challenge to social theory. Did this cultural revolution, as it appears at first glance, precede the social revolution whose economic dimension (industry based on wage labor) and political dimension (the bourgeois state, which is more or less democratic even when there are property qualifications for the franchise) took shape later? Such an interpretation of history would call into question the basic hypothesis of Marxism, since changes in the cultural factor would have determining influence over the changes in the economic and political factors. Such is the thesis of Weber—Protestantism giving birth to capitalism. But it is not my reading of this historical process, in which I see rather a concomitant transformation, in stages, of culture, the economy (mercantilism being already a transition to capitalist forms of economic organization), and politics (the absolute monarchy being already a negation of feudalism and historic compromise among feudal and bourgeois interests). This reading, I maintain, is also that of Marx.

It nevertheless remains the case that social theory can be called into question, though in a different way. The existence of proto-capitalist forms (meaning economic life in the European maritime countries during the mercantilist transition which lasted roughly from 1492 to 1789) and advanced "non-western" tributary societies (in the Indian, Chinese, and Muslim worlds, among others) during the latter Middle Ages was apparently not accompanied by a concomitant cultural transformation favorable to the completion of a capitalist social revolution. How is the exceptional nature of the route taken by Europe to be explained?

It is very tempting to explain this in culturalist terms. In the culture of this feudal and Christian Europe there would have been particular elements ("specificities") accounting for the miracle of this unique conjunction between the logics of cultural change and of economic transformation. Such a conjunction would have been absent elsewhere, because the other regions had different cultural specificities.

Culturalism emphasizes research into the specificities of that former West. This has been developed in various ways, both inside and outside the Marxist context. Within the Marxist framework, it has been suggested that the riddle could be solved through the supposition that history has proceeded along two different paths. One of these would have been governed by the so-called Asiatic mode of production which "obstructed" further evolution, while the other would have been governed by the succession from slavery to feudalism, which would have given preferential status to private forms of property (in contrast to their negation in the Asiatic mode of production) and would thus be open to change. Outside the framework of historical Marxism, other cultural analyses have given other emphases—some to the Greek ancestor of this God-favored West (reason, Prometheus, democracy), others to the merits of Christianity. In my critique of these Eurocentric constructs I have emphasized, on the one hand, what I consider the mythical nature of the "Greek ancestor" notion, and on the other, the very general flexibility of religion, a flexibility wrongly attributed to Christianity alone even though analogous examples are to be found elsewhere. Furthermore, I have noted that medieval Christianity shared with its contemporary Islam precisely that preoccupation with reconciliation between faith and reason which was to vanish in the course of the capitalist cultural revolution.

I have therefore put forward an explanation of the uniqueness of European development of a sort quite foreign to the tempting notions of culturalism. I refer to my hypothesis of unequal development throughout history, which emphasizes the flexibility of decentralized tributary modes of production (those characteristic of both feudal Europe and feudal Japan) in contrast to the rigidity of centralized tributary modes. This hypothesis, moreover, is consonant with my theme of underdetermination, in that the cultural logics of centralized tributary modes suppress those logics tending toward the development of economic opportunities, while those cultural logics weakened by the decentralized nature of other tributary modes (those which, for that reason, are rightly called feudal) yielded more easily to the requirements of economic growth.

In my view, the history of the unfinished socialist revolution, everywhere in retreat during this current phase of our epoch, confirms how important the dimension of cultural revolution is to it.

Since, in my interpretation of Marxism, socialism signifies not capitalism without capitalists, but above all a different sort of human civilization, I do not regard the call for creation of a new human being (rather than the call for "a new man," which would exclude women!) as an empty slogan. On the contrary, there will never be socialism if there are not new human beings or, to put it more modestly, if human beings do not become better and more advanced. From this becomes visible the general outline for the concept of such a new humanity: a being freer, for having transcended marketplace alienation, than one defined by the bourgeois concept of individual freedom; and a society whose workings are transparent, because such alienation has been transcended. Of course, the higher stage of socialism is not the end of history, and because of that, such transparency will remain relative. To speak of transparent economic and political decisions—within the limits of the diagram, as is said in mathematics—is to speak of an at least partial knowledge of the actual consequences of such decisions, and of a democracy enforcing such transparency; but it is also to accept the ever-present risks implicit in liberty. Within these limits, socialism conceives freedom in a much richer way than did Enlightenment philosophy.

The proposition that a new human being is necessary was not new in 1917 or in 1966 with the Cultural Revolution in China. Socialism was utopian to start with because it made that affirmation—though without offering any proof of its objective necessity. It was proclaimed in 1917. What followed was a tragedy, not a betrayal. Soviet society was not free to do what its vanguard, with its enthusiastic support, had envisaged for it. It was confronted with a problem that historic forms of Marxism had left in the shadows: that of the inherently unequal development of really existing capitalism, and thus of the inescapable need to "catch up." Gradually, it sacrificed everything to that need, which is how "the new man" became an empty slogan expressed in the stupid picture of Stakhanovites and happy collective farmers in Stalinist movies. Later, China was to run up against the same sort of problems, though its response was less of a caricature (and that is why I ascribe the depreciation of its Cultural Revolution, its placement on the level of a palace intrigue, to the absurd Eurocentrism of "Western" Marxism).

1968: another date marking the history of the project of necessary cultural revolution. That date did not come about by chance. It followed, with an unprecedentedly short two year lapse, the Cultural Revolution in China. The events of 1968 averred that Mao was right: it was first of all necessary to know how to rise in revolt, and how to do away with "leaders" (but was the cult of the Great Leader a pragmatic and circumstantial attempt to teach this, or did it go in exactly the opposite direction?); labor had to be freed from the chains of economic alienation. On those terms the project of a capitalism without capitalists, which in the last analysis is a capitalist project (with capitalists), could make way for the building of a different human civilization.

Until now there has been no common ground between these unfulfilled projects for social revolution and cultural revolution. My explanation for the distance separating them is an unremarkable one. The project of cultural revolution was in advance of its time. The major and pressing problems of Chinese society, like those of Soviet society after 1917, were more in the nature of "catching up" than of "outstripping." Resulting from the unequal development inherent in the polarizing expansion of capitalism, these agonizing problems clashed directly with the "communist utopia." Uneven development, unconsidered by historic Marxism, remained an unanswerable riddle. But it is interesting to note that these problems were to come up again elsewhere, and precisely in those metropolitan centers "corrupted by social imperialism" and "eternally" (to use "end of history" terminology) subordinated to marketplace alienation. This fundamental rejection of marketplace alienation has been reflected in major ways. It was haply recovered by Greens, by feminists, and by the new sexual and familial anarchists. Nevertheless that original rejection contributed to major changes in important aspects of social life—though only in the West!

The tragic nature of this Act One in the drama of socialist revolution is entirely to be found in this paradox: there has been no common ground until now between the forward steps of revolutionary cultural consciousness and those of the movement for a transformation in production relations. The working class movement of the Second International, and its continuation the Third, invented capitalism without capitalists. The Russian revolution, for a short moment, and, with more persistence, that of China, proclaimed their intention to go beyond that and carry out a cultural revolution. Neither one accomplished its proclaimed dream, nor, incidentally, did the West in 1968. Is the conclusion from this that communism and its new human being are hopeless utopias? Or is the conclusion that socialist revolution is a much longer process than its first actors imagined it to be?

5

From the Dominance of Economics to that of Culture: The Withering Away of the Law of Value and Problems of the Transition to Communism

Contemporary Marxist discussion needs to be expanded into new areas, whose essential questions fall under the following four headings:

First: How is the essential nature of communism, regarded as the aim of social and cultural revolution, to be defined?

Second: Has the objective evolution of modern society already posed this objective as a desirable possibility? In other words, has it already made it objectively necessary?

Third: Are the actual answers of societies to this challenge going in that direction, or, on the contrary, are they making such an evolution even more difficult?

Fourth: Under these conditions, how are we to reopen the debate over the transition from the present capitalist order to this distant objective? What strategies of progress in stages can be suggested by these considerations?

The abundance of current discourse concerning the cultural dimension of social life is a sign of the times. The extreme confusion and ambiguity of most such discourses is the result of, in the first instance, protest against the present expressed through nostalgia for the past. This applies not only to the peripheral countries, where the globalization resulting from the expansion of really existing capitalism has meant polarization to the detriment of their peoples, but likewise in the metropolitan centers whose triumphalist commercialism has been met with an ineradicable spirit of contestation, at least since 1968.

Their ambiguity stems from the fact that these protests have scarcely, until now, given rise to anything more than nostalgic views of the past, rather than a look toward the future and an attempt to put forward a universalist view of this future that would allow for the transcendence of capitalism. They suggest giving up on universalism, only just begun by capitalism, in favor of a return to the past, which is impossible and extremely dangerous. Under these conditions, the "culturalist" strategies applied by currents as diverse as communitarians and religious fundamentalists, but often also by the Greens and likewise the postmodernists, are quite co-optable and indeed have been co-opted through the main strategies of the globalized neoliberal project prevailing in the current stage. Thus it matters little that some (communitarians and postmodernists) call for a democratic respect for pluralism, or that others (ethnic and religious fanatics) proclaim their total incompatibility with differing cultures. They are all impotent to contest capitalist globalization, which in fact they accept by claiming that the real problems lie elsewhere.

Nevertheless, behind these generally very reactionary discourses is to be seen the outline of a critique of capitalism. There is nothing very new about that. Weren't some of the first utopian socialist protests against the ravages of rising capitalism expressed at the time in terms of a nostalgia for feudal times, the ambiguity of which was pointed out by Marx and Engels?

I suggest, therefore, that this preoccupation with culture has its positive side: an intuitive sense that the "better society"—which is to come, or to be built—must first of all be defined in terms of its cultural dimensions. Just as capitalism's point of departure was a reversal of the dominant factors, placing the economic factors (the law of value) above the political-ideological (the absolutist state and the metaphysical alienation validating its rationale), so communism, in my judgment, is inconceivable unless cultural (and I here emphasize that the word is cultural, not ideological) factors take the place of the economic ones (a process which I therefore call the withering away of the law of value).

Cultural, not ideological, factors must take the place of the economic and political ones, because historic Marxism put its emphasis on the political in regard to the so-called socialist transition to communism. It did so in a formulation whose ambiguity has not gone unnoticed: in the long run the withering away of the state (as the expression of the social dominance of a class) and the substitution of "the administration of things for government over men" (and over women, of course), and in the middle term, during the transition, the affirmation of the political factor, in the honorable form of Marx's commentary on the Paris Commune (the democratic dictatorship of the proletariat), and in the more dubious forms of the Soviet state and its renewal in the Maoist discourse of the Cultural Revolution (politics at the command posts).

Now, this bobtailed vision of substituting through politics a working-class political authority (the working class, or the worker-peasant bloc, or even "the whole people") for the capitalist power structure was accompanied, and not by chance, by the crystallization of a project of a "capitalism without capitalists" that was to take the concrete form of a state planned economy until that form fell apart, to give way once more to the anarchy of the marketplace. So in reality the planned economy preserved the dominance of the "economic factor," that is to say, of the law of value, as Stalin himself admitted in 1950.

The dictatorship of value—on which is based the supremacy of the economic factor—is not incompatible with a rhetoric giving pride of place to political argumentation, or to eulogies of the state and of the planning that it carries out on behalf of the people. This apparent contradiction is naturally resolved by grasping the impoverishment of that politics, which had degenerated into *"realpolitik"*—that is to say, the manipulative practices of a power structure invoking "objective requirements" (of value, or of something else, or, in sum, of anything at all). To rehabilitate the political factor requires something quite different. It involves a fundamental criticism of the dictatorship of value as the basis of the modern capitalist world's civilization and culture, and not as a basis only for those aspects of social life directly governed by economic decisions. This observation is not reserved only to the experiences of "really existing socialism." In capitalist societies political choice is just as completely denied by the brutal dictatorship of value. A rehabilitated or, in the terms of our German friends, repoliticized politics opens onto the cultural realm. It asks us to imagine a new civilization, not based on the constraints of value or on those stemming from the concepts of political power associated with it.

The supremacy of a politics that has become both our civilization and culture, that has escaped from the narrow bounds of the practices involved in exerting power, is thus synonymous with the withering away of the dictatorship of the law of value. But is that on the agenda of possibilities, the agenda of necessities objectively required by the real evolution of society?

Metamorphoses of the Law of Value

I

The simple concept of value, signifying exchange value, which in Marx is distinct from the concept of use value, signifies the presence of a social division of labor and of independent production units. Such independence does not necessarily involve either individual or collective forms of private property in land, means of production, or products of labor, even though the main historical form through which such independence has been expressed is indeed private property. But independent production units owned formally by the state and/or cooperatives can be envisaged to fulfill the same function. Thus, such independence merely requires that the "products" of these subdivided units be objects of exchange, that they have a price, which is set "freely" (within limits which could be fixed by well-understood overall legislation) through "bargaining" among the buyers and sellers of such products. Each product is then a commodity, a commercial product, whether it assumes the physical form of a "thing" or of some specific service.

There is, of course, a tangible social reality implicit in the existence of value. It can thus be grasped empirically. But, as is always the case, a deepening of scientific understanding requires us to move beyond the phenomena, beyond the appearances given directly by immediate sense-experience.

This is what distinguishes between theories of value. The empiricist method, which is clearly dominant in bourgeois philosophy, especially in the Anglo-Saxon countries, restricts itself to the phenomenal husk—in this case to the observable fact of the existence of prices—and thus reduces the theory of value to a theory of price.

Marx's method is based on the concepts of social labor and the social division of labor, whose modifications are expressed through the price mechanism. What is produced are social products, meaning that they are produced by measurable quantities of social labor. The quantity of direct and indirect social labor contained in a quantity of products can be calculated. The social division of labor is nothing but the distribution of social labor among different lines of production, and among the different independent production units making up the different branches of the social economy. Values are expressed indirectly in prices, and prices are determined by values in the last instance, but *only* in the last instance, since other factors are at play in the price structure. This is especially visible in the ownership of capital (unique to capitalism) and the relative degree of monopoly power possessed by various capitals. Marx's method takes account of the price's immediate empirical reality. The structural distribution of values has an indirect correspondence to that of prices. Values can be "transformed" into "prices of production" by adding to the conditions determining the structure of values those which express the other factors, for example the tendency toward equalization among profit rates.

Such a transformation would be seen as impossible only by those who make the mistake of using in the calculation of prices a rate of profit equal to that rate of profit which would follow directly from the rate of surplus value used in the calculation of values. I have maintained that this absurd assumption contradicts the Marxist concept of alienation, which implies that those two rates must generally be different. If they were not different, then the deeper reality would be no different from its visible reflection in the surface phenomena that manifest it, and there would be no economic-determinist alienation.

I will not belabor this point, because my present undertaking is not to defend the theory of value, within whose framework I place the ensuing discussion, but to show how the concept of value is to undergo those metamorphoses needed to lay the ground for its withering away. I pose this question and offer my response to it in terms of a withdrawal of the hypothesis that productive units are independent.

II

The law of value is expressed in the fact that commodities—meaning products of subdivided social labor—are exchanged at prices determined, in the last analysis, by values.

The law of value, therefore, is at work only when commodities exhibit two features: first, that they can be defined in terms of distinct physical quantities—for example, a yard of printed cotton fabric—and second, that they are results of social production from a production unit that is clearly distinguished from the others and has definite boundaries—in this case, for example, a weaving and printing mill that buys spun cotton and sells printed fabric. It is then indeed possible to calculate the quantity of social labor needed to turn out a single unit of the commodity at issue (I will not now go into a discussion regarding conversion of complex labor to simple labor).

Insofar as a given line of production is integrated within a firm which itself is constituted as a production unit, intermediate products all along the chain are not commodities, and therefore have neither a real value nor a real price. For example, in a textile factory that integrates the operations of spinning and weaving, the

balls of ginned cotton that it buys from other producers are in fact
commodities, having both a value and a price, but this is not so
for the spun cotton. If, outside this integrated firm, there are
independent spinning works, their spun cotton has both a value
and a price, and these can serve as reference points for the calcu-
lations by which the integrated firm evaluates its own economic
efficiency.

But what is the place of the law of value in the hypothetical case
of an organization integrating all intermediate lines of production?
Our supposition is that every distinguishable final product is the
output of a single firm which itself produces all its necessary
material inputs. In that case only the intermediary products cannot
be considered commodities. The market on which the asking price
of these final products is to be realized is a market governed by a
supply schedule representing all the different producers and a
demand schedule representing all potential consumers of such
products. Then have the subjective "preferences" of the latter
group become the decisive factor? Not at all. Were those "preferences" to require a price lower than one corresponding to value as
transformed, the integrated line of production would become
unable to realize the same rate of profitability as the others, so
capital would be diverted from it to those others, leading to a
diminution of its overproduction. The law of value would continue to govern the social distribution of labor.

In reality, this academic hypothesis is untenable, because the
interdependence among different branches of production makes
it impossible to envisage distinct, completely integrated lines of
production. For that to be the case, each line would have to include
the production of its own capital equipment. But then the social
division of labor, as envisaged among lines of production putting
out distinguishable final products, would be in contradiction to

the logic of the technological division of labor. The integration of production can only be envisaged as total, in which all technological units are embodied within a single firm—which would be a national economy, and a completely closed one at that. Then indeed all intermediate products, whether capital equipment, raw materials, or semi-finished goods, would circulate among these technological units and within each of them, but not as commodities. In contrast, the final products would retain their commodity form, for sale to consumers who would be free to buy them or not at the asking price. Thus we are back to the foregoing hypothesis. Excess inventories would signify that the price is too high, and the emergence of a black market would show that it was set too low.

There are two very different ways of envisaging the management of such an integrated economy, depending on which of two principles is called on to ensure that management.

The first principle recognizes that the social division of labor must remain based on the law of value. For this to be effective, the technological units of production must have a recognized autonomy, meaning that each must be judged according to the rate of profit that it realizes. The rate of profit realized by each such unit is determined on the basis of the reference prices used in its accounting for each unit of capital equipment or other input obtained from other units, irrespective of whether these inputs are distributed directly by a centralized organism or freely purchased. If the economic system makes use of neither subsidies nor indirect taxes, the set of prices clearing all markets for final products will determine, going back through all the lines of production, the reference prices for all the intermediate products, which prices are nothing else but transformed values. The law of value, in this case, would actually govern the social division of labor, just as it would in our previous example and does under capitalism.

The second principle rejects any need to base the social division of labor on the law of value. To put it differently, an overall planning authority would set the reference price for all inputs and, in accordance with the logic of that decision, would have to enforce their distribution among the various production units administratively. Subject to those prices, these units might or might not realize some given rate of profit. The central authority would remedy such deviations through subsidies or excess-profit taxes. The prices of final products would themselves turn out to be whatever they turned out to be at the end of the chain linking them to all the intermediate producers. They might or might not be market-clearing prices, and the central authority would in these cases also erase the deviations through subsidies or indirect taxes. This system would undoubtedly be very inefficient: some production units would find it impossible to fulfill their planned targets, while it would be made easy for others to do so. As an objective necessity, the law of value would in its own way get back at the power structure which had denied it.

III

Let us go back to really existing capitalism. Value is inherently social in a double sense. First, the output of a production unit has been made by a collective group of workers. The technological division of labor among them and the range of skills needed are determined on the basis of definite social rules, but not on the basis of the law of value. By this I mean that the salary hierarchy is not the expression of a relationship between simple and complex labor. Complex labor is that performed by a skilled worker, whose training has required a determinate time of schooling and apprenticeship, and for that reason is worth a determinate multiple of simple labor. If that relationship were to be the standard for the salary hierarchy, the latter could stand only a modest spread, perhaps on the order of 1.5 to 1, considering that the most extended training might take no more than fifteen years while the number of working years to be provided over a worker's lifetime amounts to some thirty years. In measuring the total quantity of direct and indirect labor contained in a single unit of output, this calculation must be carried out in terms of units of simple labor. From this it follows that the price of simple labor power (the base wage of an unskilled worker) is systematically lower than its value, and the price of complex labor is greater than its value. So much so, indeed, that technical and managerial personnel do not take part in the production of surplus value but, rather, share in its distribution. How is this actual hierarchy of wages to be explained? On this question, economic theory is mute or tautological. The supply and the demand for workers of different skills are themselves produced through the social production of the labor force, by means of the whole range of training systems. The claim that wages are determined by "marginal productivity" is here, as elsewhere, a tautology pure and simple. The field of operation of the law of value starts only at the firm's door, where the collective product of a group of workers becomes a commodity, a commercial product with a particular value.

Secondly, value is social because the output of any production unit is inseparable from that of all those others which provide it with capital equipment and other inputs or transport and market its products. The law of value shows how this interdependence is regulated.

Nevertheless, the social content of value is expressed through individualized supply and demand prices, meaning the prices sought by various buyers and sellers. These prices may or may not be realized, depending on many conditions specific either to the position of a particular unit or to the interaction among all such units and the conversions and diversions, the equilibria and disequilibria, resulting from those interactions.

Now this contradiction, which is to be found in all the stages of capitalist development since its start, has become greater under modern capitalism for at least three main reasons. The first is a result of the change from atomistic competition to oligopolistic competition. Monopoly carries with it a distortion of prices relative to the production prices that would express equal profit rates. This distorting effect is even more marked in that many monopolies work with long and complex chains of production. Many prices, which used to represent criteria of rationality under the workings of the law of value, have lost that significance and now have become little more than reference prices for a firm's internal accounting.

The second results from the growth of a "third department" needed to absorb the growing mass of surplus value (even though Marx, in his analysis of the process of capital accumulation, distinguished only two departments of production, a Department I producing capital goods and a Department II producing consumer goods). I will not dwell on this question, except to endorse the view first put forward by Paul Sweezy. I merely note that this third department is disparate in its makeup. It comprises, among other things, public expenditures for material objects (most of all, armaments) and for the supply of such public services as education and health care.

For its part, the service sector is heterogeneous. Some services, like some material products, are characteristically inputs for the output of final products (like transportation, marketing services, and financial services provided to enterprises) and as such must be considered as elements helping to determine the values of commodities. Others are paid for out of consumers' incomes, meaning that their production by the seller is identically an act of consumption by the buyer. There are many reasons leading to the rapid growth of the service sector in comparison to that dealing with the production of material goods.

The third reason results from the deepening of capitalist globalization. I will not dwell on this question either, which is central to the propositions that I have put forward in regard to the accumulation of capital on a world scale. I here limit myself to a restatement of my conclusion, namely that the law of value governing really existing capitalism (globalized capitalism) is not the law of value as deduced from the capitalist mode of production considered in abstraction, but is what I term the globalized law of value. This latter form brings about a systematic distortion by virtue of the fact that workers in the peripheral countries are paid at a lower rate than equally productive workers in the metropolitan centers. The global price system, which constitutes the reference point for rational capitalist economic calculation, is thus the result of a double transformation of values.

IV

At this point I will take up a new aspect of the problem of the law of value, one destined to require an additional change in the form of the law's operation. This new aspect of the problem stems from cybernetic automation. Cybernetic automation consists of the drastic reduction of direct labor—limited to the supervision and maintenance of automated equipment—in favor of indirect labor, as embodied in the production of the automated equipment. It would appear that, under the supposition that this automated machinery is itself produced through a cybernetically automated process—still an academic assumption at the current stage of technological evolution—labor itself would vanish from the picture in regard to material production. Would such a disappearance mean that value and the law of value had been wiped out, or, on the contrary, that they had become completely and perfectly socialized?

This question arises from an academic assumption of the total automation of material production at all stages—production of the automated equipment itself, of all intermediate products, and of all consumer goods.

In this case we must take into consideration four departments of production:

• Department I, accounting for the entirely automated output of means of production, automated capital equipment, and other intermediate goods and raw materials.

• Department II, producing, likewise in a completely automated way, all consumer goods.

• Department III, producing the services needed as inputs for the output of the two foregoing departments, such as research and development of new cybernetically automated production lines (a new sector of economic activity) and services of a former sort still needed for activities ancillary to production (like transportation, marketing, and financial services) though these themselves would have undergone partial cybernetic automation.

• Department IV, producing services for individual and social final consumption, themselves likewise cybernetically automated in part.

Following from the assumption of total cybernetic automation of the lines of production contained in Departments I and II, we assume that no direct labor at all is used in these sectors (though in reality a negligible amount of such labor would remain).

Additionally, we classify wage workers into two categories: ordinary workers (all of whom would now be skilled, though their skills could be ranked in some given order) and "social supervisory" workers involved in things like organization of production and decision-making. Workers in the second group are assumed to receive wages four times as large as those of workers in the first.

OUTPUTS					
INPUTS	I	II	III	IV	TOTALS
	Means of production	Final goods	Intermediate services	Final services	(in physically homogeneous units)
Means of production	P_1	P_2	P_3	P_4	P
Intermediate services	S_1	S_2	o	o	S
Ordinary labor	o	o	L_3	L_4	L
Social supervisory labor	L'_1	L'_2	L'_3	L'_4	L'

The lines of this table are to be read as follows:

First line: goods for intermediate consumption (raw materials and cybernetically automated machinery), expressed in physical units and apportioned among the four Departments (P1, P2, P3, P4).

Second line: services for intermediate consumption, expressed in service units and apportioned between Departments I and II (S1, S2).

Third line: apportionment of ordinary labor, expressed in millions of workers per year, all of whom are occupied in the service-producing Departments (L3 and L4) inasmuch as the lines of production of material goods are all assumed to be completely automated.

Fourth line: Allocation of social supervisory labor, expressed in millions of workers per year and apportioned among the four sectors.

To each physical unit we assign an average price per unit, as follows:

- price per unit of capital goods p1
- price per unit of means of consumption p2
- price per unit of intermediate services p3
- price per unit of final services p4
- annual wage of an ordinary worker . . . . w
- annual wage of a social supervisory worker

  . . . . w'=kw (k=4 as assumed)

$\sim$

VALUES					
INPUTS	I	II	III	IV	TOTALS
	Means of production	Final goods	Intermediate services	Final services	(in value terms)
Means of production	P_1p_1	P_2p_1	P_3p_1	P_4p_1	Pp_1
Intermediate services	S_1p_3	S_2p_3	0	0	Sp_3
Ordinary labor	0	0	L_3w	L_4w	Lw
Social supervisory labor	L'_1w'	L'_2w'	L'_3w'	L'_4w'	$L'w'$

• The output of means of production, given as the total of the first column (P1p1+S1p3+L'1w') is taken up by the demand from all four Departments (Pp1, the total of line I).

• The output of intermediate services, given as the total of the third column (P3p1+L3w+L'3w') corresponds to the demand for it, given as the total of the second line (Sp3).

• The income distributed as wages (Lw+L'w') is sufficient to take up the total output of final goods (P2p1+S2p3+L'2w' in the second column) and services (P4p1+L4w+L'4w in the fourth column).

The purpose of this exercise is not to discuss the conditions needed for the system of linear equations expressing an equilibrium to be consistent (an inconsistent system has no solution), determinate (meaning that there is only one set of prices at which the system would be at equilibrium), or indeterminate (permitting an infinite number of solutions). Neither is it to discuss the eventual possibility of carrying out a suitable aggregation, and even less so is it to discuss whether or not any system of linear equations like this can reconcile the approaches of microeconomics and macroeconomics. Indeed, my general view is that the workings of economic rationality, by themselves, do not lead to the sought-for equilibrium, and still less do they lead to a stable equilibrium. Thus, if more-or-less stable equilibria should actually occur, they would in any case do so through a combination (simultaneously complementary and contradictory) of economic logic with other, ineradicable, social and political logics. This is why pure economics' quest for proofs represents an absurd undertaking, and its ambition to take the place of historical materialist analysis is an empty one.

The purpose of the exercise is merely to give an illustration of the metamorphoses to which the evolution of the economic system subjects the very concept of value, whose increasing socialization calls into question the notion of strictly economic rationality.

Cybernetic automation is a challenge to the concept of value and to the law of value, for social supervisory labor does not represent, according to its main characteristics, a direct or indirect contribution to the productive labor process. It is a matter of the usage of surplus value.

In the value table, the national income amounts to $Lw + L'w'$, with Lw representing the wages of ordinary workers. The surplus value—in this case $L'w'$—is henceforward allocated in the form of wages to the managers and executives who organize production, supervise it, and profit from it. This new form of compensation to capital takes the place of the earlier form in which profit is allocated in proportion to the relative share of the social capital controlled by each firm. In our model, there is no bar to the possibility that, in practice, oligopolistic firms would set the price for their output by adding up the cost of inputs and of their labor force, and adding to it a compensation for capital (proportional to the latter, but at a variable rate depending on competitive circumstances). This amount would in reality be apportioned among its managers and executives in the form of salaries, while the net profit remaining after this distribution would be negligible (in our table it amounts to zero). Note that this overall surplus value includes a surplus (in the Sweezy-Baran sense) which here would be taken up in the form of consumption of final services, in part by individuals but above all collectively (through public expenditures).

Since the industries producing material goods, considered apart from other industrial sectors, make use of no productive labor, no exploitation of labor takes place within them because no new labor is embodied in their output; they make use only of indirect labor embodied in the output of intermediate services (basic research and research and development of cybernetically automated equipment). Exploitation of labor would reappear only were one to consider the economy as aggregating Departments I, II, and III. But even on that level only a small minority of workers would be linked to the production of material goods. Most exploited workers would be engaged in the output of final services, some of which would go directly to individual consumers and others to the surplus-absorbing public expenditures. These workers thus would not be exploited in production, though their social status would be comparable to those exploited in the traditional sense of the word.

What would take place, then, is that the principal form of exploitation would become manifest through the overall distribution of income. The meaning of value would then be found only at this integrated and comprehensive level, the social product being divided between a proletariat of ordinary workers and a bourgeoisie of social supervisors. Of course, so vast a metamorphosis of the concept of value would have huge ideological significance and critical social and political effects.

The concept of value would subsist, but only because society would still be dominated by economic determinist alienation. This would bring us back to Marx's starting point, the linkage of value and marketplace alienation. This alienation could be wiped out only by an alternative vision and practice in the administration of things, whereby social supervisors would truly be agents of social control—which signifies the organization of a really democratic social power structure, whereby overall production priorities would really be set by the collectivity and no longer by decisions made in its name by a minority (which, into the bargain, pays itself, and very well indeed) pretending to legitimacy on the basis of its ability to make the economy conform to the requirements of economic law.

As long as this is not the case, the system would still be governed by a transformed law of value, operating through competition among the dominant oligopolistic firms.

Through its internal evolution, capitalism socializes the production process, but it does so without by itself being able to take the final step required to accomplish this socialization: the transformation of the political, ideological, and social system into a democracy emancipated from marketplace alienation. Only this transformation deserves to be considered a passage to socialism. If this transformation does not occur, then a "socialized" system would in all important aspects resemble that described above, a system on the assumption that all firms are completely integrated with each other, having lost their autonomy as property of a state whose absolute monopoly power would make it the essential form of the contrast between proletarian and bourgeois classes.

Of course, this hypothetical case is clearly the Sovietist system: capitalism without capitalists, or, to put it more precisely, a capitalism in which the bourgeoisie is established as one single capitalist.

In conclusion: reflections on the transition beyond capitalism

In the conclusion of my recent book, *Capitalism in the Age of Globalization* (London: Zed Press, 1996), I discussed the transition question at sufficient length that I need not dwell here on the argument already put forward in that context. At this point I need merely recall that, having defined historic capitalism by three basic contradictions proper to it (economic alienation, global polarization, destruction of the natural environment) which together characterize its specific mode of exploiting labor, I maintained that a transition beyond capitalism could begin when a project of social transformation is set in motion that, through its political economy, its politics, and its culture, would orient social evolution toward reducing these contradictions rather than permanently aggravating them. In contrast to the traditional forms of transition hitherto advanced by historical socialist movements, I propose a long transition during which, within a single society, in terms of both its national components and its global dimensions, forces tending to reproduce the characteristics of capitalism would clash with oppositely oriented forces that could well be termed antisystemic.

The transition strategy that I propose is not voluntarist, in the accepted meaning of that term (as synonymous with "unrealistic"); rather it is based on the idea that history is always open to differing possibilities, that it has room for equally possible alternative choices whose confrontation in the field of real struggles and projects for social change is the basis for their credibility and legitimacy. This field of possibility—which, I maintain, defines objective necessity in the Marxian sense—follows from the idea of underdetermination which I elaborated in Chapter Three.

Accordingly, discussion of the conditions for this particular (desirable) possibility must not be mixed up with discussion bearing on the differing alternative futurist scenarios. This latter discussion certainly is itself also a necessary one, because it brings us back to considering how the forces clashing today in the field of real struggles are shaping the future. In this regard, it is not surprising to see extremely diverse and even contradictory hypotheses advanced by various discussants, and often with weighty arguments.

The most pessimistic of visions is that one which would practically wipe out any room for the construction of a human civilization different from that governed by the inherent laws of capitalism, specifically the three contradictions pointed out above. In this perspective, history just goes on along its well-beaten track, or, in other words, capitalism constitutes, as far as the eye can see, the bounds of possible evolution, the "end of history" as Francis Fukuyama ingenuously claimed. This evolution, projected forward, yields the apocalyptic vision of *pure war*, an inexorable advance toward the extinction of the human race. No less uneasily, but with a greater number of positive arguments, Michel Beaud has shown (and his exposition is all too convincing) that the political economy of technological science based on established social relations—the capitalist economic logics driving giant enterprises that are essentially transnational oligopolies, the cultural forces serving to replicate marketplace alienation, and the political means, even partially democratic ones, whereby these forces act effectively—is far from having used up its potential destructiveness of humanity and the natural environment. I really believe this to be not only one possibility, albeit one possibility among several, but also the very one presently materializing, and the worst imaginable possibility to boot.

Coming down a notch, still looking to move from the abstract toward the concrete, we then pose precise questions, such as:

First, are we to see new centers, in the image of those we know today, become established in a diminution of polarization that offers no challenge to economic alienation and environmental destruction?

Second, are we heading toward convergence of the metropolitan centers (on the path toward underdevelopment, to put it briefly) with the peripheral countries (on the capitalist development path, to keep the same language), producing a homogenizing globalization which would be prelude either to a surpassing of its capitalist content (in the optimistic hypothesis) or (in the pessimistic hypothesis) to its ineluctable procession toward barbarism and death?

As I have already said, the arguments of the various parties are not negligible ones. It is not an uninteresting academic question to ask whether, in the economies which currently seem to be on the high road toward success (especially in East Asia), the islands of modernization will succeed in steadily reducing the area of "underdevelopment" surrounding them, or whether they will stay isolated, replicating in a new form the subordination and fragmentation defining peripheral status in a polarized global system. Nor is it to enter on a futile debate to ask whether one or the other of these outcomes is the more likely, in the specific instance either of the mid-sized countries (South Korea, Taiwan, tomorrow perhaps Malaysia or Thailand) or of the giants (China, tomorrow India). On the contrary, these questions are the obligatory starting point for a broader debate. I will not offer here a detailed discussion of the economic arguments that have been advanced on these matters. I limit myself to a restatement of my outlook, which is that there are only very weak chances of a positive outcome—new centers taking shape—for the reasons that I put forward to emphasize the "five monopolies" of the metropolitan centers, their replication and aggravation of capitalist polarization under new forms. Of course, this viewpoint is also that of others, whose concrete analyses lend strength to my position (cf. Yoshikara Kunio and Diana Hochraich).

At the other extreme of the spectrum in regard to these hypotheses, Alain Lipietz and Giovanni Arrighi put forward the notion that the most recent phase of globalization is bringing the models of metropolitan and peripheral countries closer to each other. At the moment when a neoliberal offensive is proceeding to dismantle the welfare state in both Europe and the United States, there is nothing theoretical about the hypothesis of a regression from Fordist regulation to a deregulated Taylorism based on competitiveness acquired through reduction of wages. It is going on. Is it turning the United States into another Brazil, as Lipietz has the fortunate (fortunate because thought-provoking) boldness to suggest? Arrighi likewise has stated that globalization has restored the commonality between the active labor force and the reserve army of the unemployed, which are now no longer separated geographically and politically but are both present in metropolitan and peripheral countries alike. I will also not give further consideration here to these views, which I have discussed elsewhere. I consider them to be too much under the influence of short term actualities, which they extrapolate further than is warranted. I strongly hold that those societies which have attained the level of mass consumption have considerable powers of resistance to this new retrogradation. All the same, there are troubling exceptions: for a century now, hasn't Argentina been an example that continual retrogression is possible? But my argument goes further: the economic model linked to such retrogressive evolution would shut capitalism into a permanent slump and financial crisis. This fact makes it untenable. It therefore creates conditions for renewed struggle against the logics on which it is based. Would those struggles confront economic alienation, would they rebel against global polarization and destruction of the natural environment? Such an outcome is possible.

And thus we are brought back to our most important concern: what are the preconditions for inception of the long transition beyond capitalism?

The technological revolution (computerization and cybernetic automation) has already initiated a metamorphic process for exchange value, opening the possibility of the withering away of its dictatorial sway. The ongoing socialization of the labor process has already reached a level where the law of value has begun to exhaust its economic rationality as distributional norm and measure of wealth, as we are reminded by Farida Sebai and Carlo Vercellone, who quite appropriately refer to the notion of a "general intellect," which Marx conceived a century before its time. Objective circumstances compel recognition of the idea of a citizenship income, which would take the place of wages paid to the sellers of labor power. As Andre Gorz put it: "People will no longer receive income in proportion to the quantity of labor furnished by them, but rather in proportion to the quantity of wealth that society decides to produce. . . . Payment will no longer be made for labor and to workers, but for living and to citizens."

But the question here arises: what sort of "citizen" is to receive such income? It is most tempting to define citizenship income with reference to the political state, since the means for its eventual achievement will have to be worked out within that framework. Nevertheless, such a restriction clashes with the globalization of value. This globalization, even incomplete, weakens the autonomy of any productive system and thus limits the scope and efficacity of the interdependent mechanisms at work within it. Value already has a globalized dimension, even despite the bobtailed market in which it is manifest. In concrete terms, would real incomes in the metropolitan countries be as high as they are if access to the resources of the whole planet had not been arranged to the exclusive profit of their citizens? In this sense, the citizenship at issue has already become a universal citizenship. Citizenship income will have to be conceived, at least in part, as destined for all the human beings on this planet. National citizenship incomes will thus have to be linked to a worldwide redistribution of wealth, power, and value.

Founded on the three historical compromises signified at the time by the welfare state in the West (social-democratic and Keynesian forms of Fordist regulation), Sovietism in the East, and the project of nationalist development in the South, the strategies put into play during the postwar phase (1945-1985) were all based on an expanding arena for the law of value. This is striking in the case of the welfare state, whose growth was based on the growth of value-governed output. It was no less true of the modernization projects in the South, and likewise so for Sovietism, even though in the latter case the dictatorship of value was masked by the statified planned economy.

The strategies to be envisaged for the future, a future that starts today, cannot be mere remakes of those past strategies. They must be based, from the very outset and in all regions of the world, on the expansion of unmercantile social activities. It is under this—and only this—perspective that we can envisage both a controlled globalization (beginning a shrinkage of polarization and thus a North-South cooperation worthy of the name) and a serious regard for what is required to protect the natural basis of life on this planet. Only in this perspective does sustainable development have any meaning.

6

Postmodernism—A Neoliberal Utopia in Disguise?

I

In Chapter Two, I offered an interpretation of the successive modes in which the dominant ideology of our modern capitalist societies has been expressed. I chose to arrange my propositions around a central axis supplied by the political economy of the capitalist system. The kernel providing continuity to this economic discourse is exemplified by the liberal utopia, according to which the market is not merely the congenial regulator of modern social life but also is self-regulating, in the sense that it can go on working by itself without the need of external forces to structure its operations. But the ideology of capitalist political economy is expressed in this crude and extreme form only under exceptional circumstances. In reality, the operations of really existing capitalism are regulated by two series of factors foreign to that unilateral logic: the balance of forces among different social classes, around which is structured the capital/labor contradiction that is the permanent defining characteristic of the system; and the relationships among the different national participants making up the global capitalist system. All of these relationships are in permanent flux, and thus mark in their distinctive way each successive stage of modern history. For capitalist political economy to be efficacious, that is to say, for it to make a positive contribution to the reproduction of the system, it must be continually adapted to the objective requirements expressed by these relationships. With this as a starting point, I therefore suggested an interpretation of the history of the dominant ideology as a series of successive discourses, whose types I have termed liberal nationalist, then social and national, and finally globalized neoliberal.

In focusing attention on this essential dimension of the analysis, I am not claiming that the social thought of any given period could be reduced to it. On the contrary, social thought is inherently multidimensional, because it must take all aspects of social life into consideration. Social thought splits up, in order to spread into particular fields, according to the individual nature of each of its aspects. The progress of knowledge comes at this price, providing meticulous and intelligent observation of the real world in all the complexity of its manifestations. But at every point there remains the question of how consistent with each other are the conclusions drawn from the progress of knowledge in each sector. Does the acquired knowledge remain fragmented, with no hope of getting beyond that stage? Or does it allow for a recombination, which would rearticulate each of these types of knowledge into a single architecture, giving them new strength drawn from the holistic perspective to which they are linked?

The answer to this perpetual question pertains to philosophy. All philosophical systems throughout the ancient world were structured around a metaphysical form of this problem: there is a governing cosmic order which imposes itself on human beings and on their societies. Their task, at best, was to seek out the divine commandments holding sway over them, or else to learn them through the utterances of prophets.

The modern era began with a philosophical break from that past. An era of freedom, but also of insecurity, began. Once political power was stripped of divine sanction, and the natural world was stripped of magical influences, the way to the free exercise of human reason was opened. Henceforth humanity was called to the knowledge that human beings make their own history, that they can and even must do so, and that to do so they must choose. The modern world is defined by this rupture through which humanity escapes from the commandments of a cosmic order—frees itself, rather, in the view of those who, like myself and many others, see this rupture as progress. For my part, it must be said that in the past metaphysical alienation was a necessary requirement for the reproduction of those precapitalist social systems which I have characterized as tributary, and the overstepping of this alienation is linked to the social system's qualitative transformation into a capitalist one. I insist on the word "overstepping" (*dépassement*) rather than "abolition," because I maintain that in its transhistorical, anthropological dimension the human being is a metaphysical animal. But that is a different question, not to be discussed here.

To overstep metaphysics is thus to assert that there is a dichotomy between nature and society, and by that fact to reject any confusion between the domain governed by natural laws (whose discovery is the business of the natural sciences) and that governed by "societal" laws. Recognizing that such laws, because humanity makes its own history, have a status different from that of natural laws, I now, as always, insist on this distinction, which is a subject of perpetual discussion. For it is not accepted by those for whom the natural sciences represent the model to which the social sciences are to be approximated. Because I consider such an approximation to be both a distortion and an impossibility, I have suggested that we should speak of social thought rather than social science, without for a moment conceding that this terminology implies that a scientific worldview is dispensable in the investigation of social thought.

For me there is no other definition of modernity, and modernity requires nothing more than the philosophical rupture to which I have referred. Thus we see that modernity can never be completed, never be closed. To the contrary, it opens onto the unknown, whose boundaries, though ultimately unattainable, are pushed ever further backward in step with the accumulation of our knowledge in regard to the social realm. Modernity is unending. But it takes on a succession of forms, which vary according to the responses it offers to the challenges confronting society at each moment of its history.

At every instant, modern social thought is torn between its aspiration to treat human beings as the free authors of their own history and its recognition that they are subject to seemingly objective laws comparable to the laws of nature. Under capitalism, the dominance of economic factors is expressed as the autonomy of economic forces. Like natural forces, these act as realities answering to objective laws. In the dominant discourse there is a perpetual insistence on a supposedly unavoidable submission to these notorious economic laws (which vulgarizing rhetoric encapsulates in the phrase "the market"). In vaguer and often cruder forms of this rhetoric, reference is made to laws of nature, and even to a "state of nature," to which people would be as subject as they are to objective forces. Recall, however, that in the Enlightenment modernity defined itself, with its call to escape from supposedly natural laws and to give full authority to the lawmaking citizen. But as we will see, retrogression toward submission to these alleged demands of nature is always lurking in the recesses of bourgeois thought. From nineteenth-century social Darwinism to aggressive contemporary insistence on genetic and "neurological" explanations of social phenomena, this deviant conceit is perpetually present. Yet it is forcefully expressed only under certain conditions, and therefore it is essential to specify them.

The proposition according to which humanity makes its own history represented the birth process of modernity and defined the field of inquiry for social thought but suggested no answers to such interrogation. Who is the active agent of this history: all individuals, or only some of them? Social classes? Various communities and groups with their own unique qualities and statuses? Nations? Societies organized as political states? And how is this history made? What real factors do these agents put to work? What strategies do they adopt, and why? How, and according to what criteria, do they judge success? What real conditions are transformed by their activities? To what extent do those transformations correspond to the goals of their authors, and to what extent do they diverge? All these questions remain perpetually open. They simply remind us that modernity is a permanently moving process, not a system that is closed and defined once and for all.

The movement of history is not foreknown. It does not proceed along a straight line and in a single direction. It is made up of moments of advance in some direction, of hesitations, of retreats, of blind alleys, of choices at forking pathways.

During periods of tranquil progress, it is always very tempting to think of the historical process in linear terms. These are periods which the political economy of the system interprets as phases of accumulation ensuring reproduction of the social relations primary to the system. During those moments, history seems to be going, naturally and inevitably, in a foreknown direction. Those are moments during which social thought seems capable of producing powerful and coherent doctrines, those of the "great narratives" (such as the bourgeois democratic project, the socialist project, or nation-building projects) which current social thought, in deep crisis, treats as objects of ridicule. There was no difficulty in giving each special branch of knowledge, as it applied to its own plot in the field of social reality, its appropriate place within such an architectonic doctrine.

On the other hand, when the social equilibria that hitherto had ensured the calm reproduction of society have turned topsy turvy, when no one can foresee the direction in which society will move once its equilibria have been restored, the crisis also becomes manifest in the collapse of those big, reassuring, intellectual structures. Their weak points become yawning gaps. Such periods are then marked by the fragmentation of social thought, and this fragmentation provides fodder for wayward conceits that direct it away from its needed reconstruction.

Since my interpretation of contemporary history treats it as having moved out of a period of the former sort which foundered in the current crisis, I will undertake here to finish off the analysis of the successive ideological modes of capitalist political economy, which I outlined in Chapter Two, with an analysis of the evolution of social thought in its other dimensions, proposing an interpretation of the ongoing decomposition of the forms modernity took during the postwar era.

II

Is modernity outlived, as is complacently uttered in current fashionable discourse? Not in the least. For if modernity simply means that human beings make their own history, then it is a long way from becoming outlived. Undoubtedly, in times of deep crisis like the present, there is a great temptation to go back to a premodern stance and claim that while human beings believe that they make their own history, in reality history takes place quite apart from their activity. In other words, there is a temptation to claim that what happens goes in no direction that anyone can even discover, let alone hope to influence by constructive and consequential action, and accordingly to suggest falling back on the unambitious stance of trying to manage this meaningless history as well as possible. To manage as well as possible, then, means the democratic administration of pluralism at the grass-roots level, the organization of so-called "conviviality," the improvement of this or that aspect of social life. The counterpart to this is acceptance of the essential features of the established system, including the rule that the market dominates everything—i.e., capitalist political economy. The motives leading to these conclusions are understandable: they stem from disarray consequent to the exhaustion and even collapse of the great projects marking the preceding stage of history, especially the socialist project but also that of the nation-state and various others. But to understand these motives is not the same thing as to believe that this situation might last, let alone that it will last forever as is proclaimed in the "end of history" thesis.

Now I maintain that the viewpoint known as postmodernism can be entirely summed up in those few foregoing lines. The basic idea of modernity—that human beings make their own history— in no way means that at every moment of its history humanity, whether as a whole or through some fractions of itself, acts in conformity with the logical requirements of a project shaping the direction in which history "must go or can go," nor that this project (or these clashing projects) will take effect. That would be to read too much into this proposition, even though it is true that a temptation to do so not only exists but even has manifested forcefully at certain moments in the course of history. The fundamental proposition of modernity means nothing more than that social action can give a meaning to history, and that it is desirable that it should do so.

Moreover, a negative attitude toward this latter proposition, which is the stance of postmodernism, is untenable. And this is why societies are never content to be consigned to a situation in which only small short-term improvements are possible. Postmodernism as a theory is accompanied in reality by far more powerful movements calling for retrogression to a premodern condition.

Islamic fundamentalism provides the most drastic example of this appeal, since it dares to go so far as to claim that there can be no lawgiver but God and that society must renounce any attempt to choose under what laws it will be governed. I have elsewhere said that this attitude stems from a major historical defeat suffered by the societies in which it becomes manifest. The consequence is that these societies are shut into a blind alley by such renunciation, which signifies rejection of the need to diagnose the origin of that defeat, to size up the real challenges besetting these societies, and to bend to the need to invent ways to confront those challenges. This attempt to "step outside of history" can only confine these societies into an inexorably descending spiral toward marginalization on a global scale, leading the way to even worse defeats. To "step outside history" is not a response only of Muslim societies, nor is it a new one. This crazy ambition occurs whenever reaction takes over the foreground, as often follows the retreat of a revolutionary tide. In Restoration France, for example, Joseph de Maistre proclaimed that the liberatory aspiration of the Revolution was a chimera to be abandoned, that the lawmaking madness of modern democracy was to be renounced because "only God is a legitimate lawgiver," and that the tradition of respect for God's law was to be dutifully obeyed at all times and in all places.

Under less serious circumstances the postmodernist refusal takes on different demeanors, less tragic, perhaps, but not less negative: by taking refuge in national, subnational, and ethnic communities they testify to this daily. Now, these retreats go exactly counter to the sincere wishes of the postmodernists for a strengthening of democratic practices in the administration of everyday affairs. They give fodder to conformity and hatred, to contempt for democracy, and to all sorts of chauvinisms (cf. Samir Amin, *L'Ethnie à l'assaut des nations* [Ethnicity's onslaught against the nations], L'Harmattan 1994; partly published in English, Chapter Four in *Capitalism in the Age of Globalization*, London: Zed Press, 1996).

Postmodernism, therefore, is a negative utopia (in contradistinction to positive utopias, which call for transformation of the world). At bottom, it expresses capitulation to the demands of capitalist political economy in its current phase, in the hope— the utopian hope—of "humanely" managing the system. This position is untenable.

Preceding the postmodernist propositions is an extensive rhetoric asserting "the failure of modernity." The least that can be said on the topic is that this superficial discourse has no analytic foundation whatsoever. The modern epoch is also the epoch of humanity's greatest achievements, accomplished at a pace immeasurably greater than that which marked premodern times. Modernity achieved enormous progress in material production and scientific knowledge; likewise, progress of democracy despite its limits and occasional setbacks; social progress, also despite its limits; and even ethical progress. The idea that each human life is irreplaceable, the idea of happiness, the idea of individuality irreducible to membership in a familial or ethnic collectivity— these are all modern ideas. Certainly these results of progress—and I have no qualms about using that currently unfashionable word— did not come about through continuous movement along a straight line; they had to be won, they are always threatened, and there are setbacks which are always accompanied by enormous crimes. But this is no reason to throw out the baby with the bathwater and to mutter "things used to be better." Nor is it a reason to simply say that because of "failures" we must give up on the foolhardy struggle to go forward and instead be content to simply cope with the present reality—that would be to take a leap which I consider neither necessary nor useful.

It is senseless to claim, as some have done, that modernity is "bankrupt" because it is to blame for Auschwitz. Hitler, an open enemy of all Enlightenment thought, was no product of the Enlightenment. Hitler undertook to wipe out the greatest conquests of the Enlightenment, the concepts of democracy and citizenship, and to replace them with a primitive communalist New Order. It would make at least as much sense to say that Hitler was the result of Christianity, since Nazism developed in a Christian country, or that he was the product of the white race or of Aryan genes. Facile polemical arguments like these have no weight in any serious analysis. But their bearing has been promptly grasped precisely by those who are enemies of democracy, inspired by nostalgia for the times that came before the Enlightenment. Christian and Muslim fundamentalists, among others, immediately seized on them, proclaiming, "You see that we were right all along to say that modernity is worthless and that we must go back to the traditional order of things." The confusion that feeds on this sort of rhetoric has results exactly opposite to those hoped for by the postmodernists!

Modernity is still unfinished, and it will remain so as long as the human race continues to exist. Currently, the fundamental obstacle setting its limits is still defined by the social relationships specific to capitalism. What the postmodernists refuse to see is that modernity can progress further only by going beyond capitalism. Unfortunately this possibility seems inaccessible at the present moment. For the "failures" of modernity and the aggravation of conflict that has brought with it that wave of violence—recognition of which is the source of the postmodernist thesis—are results of the evolution of that same capitalism and signs that it has reached the end of the historical path at whose earlier stages it could still, despite its specific contradictions, appear synonymous with progress. Today the choice "socialism or barbarism" is truly the choice confronting the human race.

Postmodernism draws no distinctions in its indictment of the various "great narratives." It rejects the concept of capitalism which, like Enlightenment, it treats as synonymous with reason and modernity. Undoubtedly, all these great narratives are based on a single abstract notion, that of emancipation—another way of saying that human beings make their own history—and accordingly they seek to formulate concretely liberatory projects. The Enlightenment established that the concepts of reason and emancipation are closely corresponding, even synonymous, with each other: reason becomes meaningless if it is not put to the service of emancipation, and the latter is impossible if it is not based on the former. Nevertheless, this common denominator is not a sufficient basis to mix up the bourgeois-democratic project with the socialist project, whose objective is precisely the overstepping of the limits of the bourgeois-democratic project. The bourgeois-democratic project was liberatory of the citizen and the individual through the establishment of a law-governed state and universal education, but was deferential to such fundamental requirements of capitalism as property, entrepreneurship, wage labor, and the laws of the market. Nor can one be content with mentioning the failures of each project (mass culture and the associated manipulation of democratic process under capitalism, the deviant course that drove the Sovietist project onto the rocks) to justify the conclusion that it is no longer possible to give meaning to history. No doubt the question remains open as to who is to be the agent of such a historic vision. Nothing says that this agent must be the same in all circumstances and at all times (for example, the proletariat). Neither does anything say that the liberatory project must at its very inception set itself final goals ("right away," as the 1968 slogan put it) and ignore the real challenges delimiting the necessary choices among transitional stages.

We must go further. For it is true that to proclaim that human beings make their own history was likewise to put an end to the security—or, rather, the false security—yielded by the previous metaphysic of cosmic order. There is no riskless freedom. That is why the modern world could produce, in parallel fashion, the best and the worst. The Frankfurt School, confronting Nazism and Stalinism, focused attention on this dialectical contradiction specific to modernity. This thinking must be taken seriously, despite its unfortunate distortion in the currently fashionable facile postmodern rhetoric. The Enlightenment produced the law-governed state, but also de Sade (and likewise Nietzsche), whose writings, though they can certainly be interpreted in diverse ways, do include a panegyric to violence. To combat freedom, the defenders of the moral order have always made use of its contradictions. But *carnalitas*—to use a word suggested by Yves Benot—does not result from the modern world. It is a transhistorical dimension of the human race. It existed before the modern epoch, even though defenders of the moral order do all they can to hide that fact. A better understanding of this *carnalitas*—and surrealism, Freudianism, and modern feminism have certainly contributed to such understanding—is still needed, precisely in order to combat, or at least limit, its effects. The facts are there to prove that the dangers attendant to "excessive freedom" (including sexual freedom) are infinitely less catastrophic than those afflicting more repressive societies. In such societies (like those of the Arabian peninsula), all sorts of barbaric violence are indeed far more common than in the "West" which they condemn as "morally decadent." The moral order never is effective. Vive la liberté!

It is likewise important not to get the intentions of liberatory projects mixed up with general theories that explain the workings of society. It is true that the latter carry conviction only during phases favorable to the development of the former, and that they become broadly unconvincing during phases of social crisis. It is, accordingly, the case that during the postwar phase antecedent to our current crisis such general theories, as diverse as structuralism, functionalism, and Sovietist Marxism, won large followings. The fact remains that the status of these theories was not at all the same. Those which were linked to mainstream bourgeois thought undertook to explain society, but not to transform it. This was the case with functionalism and structuralism. They share that fundamental position with all the other tendencies of bourgeois thought, including postmodernism—it is for this reason that they deserve to be qualified as bourgeois social thought. Capitalism appears appropriate to them, even seems to represent in a certain way the end of history, because it appears to them that it cannot ever be overstepped. Such is obviously not the case with Marxism, which to be sure undertakes to explain society, but also undertakes to transform it. Nevertheless, this characteristic, which makes it qualitatively different from other currents in social thought, confers by itself no immunity against errors and inadequacies in its analyses of reality and, consequently, in the transformative strategies that it puts forth. Like every form of social thought, it must itself be subject to continuous critical examination, and confront the challenges of the real world. This critical examination must therefore place historical forms of Marxism in the framework of the conditions that gave birth to them, exactly as is the case for tendencies within bourgeois thought. In this framework, then, Sovietist Marxism finds its place alongside other social theories.

Moreover, there is nothing that says that the failure of Sovietism was the failure of socialism, yesterday, today, or tomorrow. Without denying their reality or minimizing their scope, these failures can be analyzed in a quite different way—which I consider more precise and scientific—not by treating them as consequences of the supposedly absurd notion of emancipation, but by linking them to the concrete history of really existing capitalism. In this perspective the failure of Sovietism finds its appropriate position: not the failure of socialism but failure of the project of building a particular form of capitalism (capitalism without capitalists) under particular conditions accounting for that failure (the uneven development of global capitalism).

Modernity dons multiple shapes, be they successive or coincident, complementary or contradictory. This is why I maintain that it is inadequate to resort to the prefixes "neo" and "post" to indicate its moments, its aspects, or its formulations. This use—or, rather, abuse—usually reflects an inadequate analysis, unable to account for the causes for the success of, or putting an end to the forms of modernity at issue. I therefore prefer to set forth a critical history of modern social thought, in order to put into a proper relationship its formulations, on the one hand, and the challenges of the real world and the way in which they are perceived, on the other.

III

From this point of view, much is to be learned from the series of fashions that have held the American stage. The United States, throughout the postwar era, seems to have held a lead which made its fashions set the tone for the tendencies which would be preponderant on a world scale. As early as 1959 C. Wright Mills wrote, in *The Sociological Imagination*, "we are entering the postmodern period." And the causes he assigned for this are the same that would reappear in France, a quarter century later, from the postmodernist pen: the double failure of modernity signified, in his view, by the submergence of Western society in mass culture (with its associated manipulation of the democratic process) and bloodsoaked Stalinist dogmatism.

The form of modernity propounded in the United States during the 1950s was a simple, unpuzzling one, easily explained by the postwar boom: the diminution of social conflict (full employment), the advance of suburbanization, and the even more prodigious growth in secondary and higher education opened the way to unprecedented growth of the middle classes (the "standard model consumer/citizen"). Despite leftist protests (notably that of Mills) against the mass culture resulting from this system, and rightist protests against the "unbearable" impositions of an allegedly bureaucratic state, this model not only won general acceptance but was exported as well (into Europe, and even, after a fashion, into the post-Stalin U.S.S.R.). It laid the groundwork for a supposed theory of modernization which in turn set the pattern for the projects of third world development.

The realities of capitalist expansion during this phase (mass culture, colonial wars) resulted, as we know, in the explosion of the 1960s, culminating in 1968 which put an end to the modernizers' self-confidence. By virtue of its call for more freedom at all levels, the movement gained far-reaching progressive impact. 1968 was the inception of profound transformations in very diverse areas of culture, ideology, and social life, which spread out during the succeeding decades and have not yet exhausted their potential even though, under present circumstances, they have become the object of powerful reactionary counteroffensives. However, 1968 did not succeed in giving shape to a new overall project. My explanation for this is that it ran up against the false countermodel of Sovietist dogmatism, which had not yet become exhausted, despite Maoist critiques (which had widespread appeal in the West at that time) whose inadequacies can be explained (even though after the event) by a combination of the objective conditions of Chinese society and the inadequacies of historical Marxism.

The stage, then, was set for postmodernist ideas to find a facile resonance in society. The reaction to what was experienced as the double failure of modernity (in reality, failure of capitalist expansion) and of its critique in practice (circumscribed by the burden of Sovietism) easily lent conviction to the call for relatively limited projects and actions which would be all that was possible in the short run.

At present it seems that, while this postmodernist discourse continues to spread in Europe, it has already run out of gas in the United States. Its successor, neomodernism, retains some of the major aspects of postmodernism, especially its doctrinal fragmentation and its judgmental relativism. But at the same time it may be that neomodernism, by openly going over to the central theses of neoliberalism, has unmasked the role of postmodernism, which is to express the demands of the logic of the political economy of the current globalized neoliberal stage. The fragility of that stage leads me to think that neither postmodernism nor neomodernism has much of a future. We will return to this question.

The current postmodernist mentality is receptive and tolerant, which is certainly no defect but rather an appreciable advantage. Its sense of relativism and its mistrust of big holistic theoretical structures have favored innovation in various hitherto unexplored or little-studied fields and the invention of new, avant-gardist methodologies. These things are to the credit of our times. But their counterpart is a fear of making mistakes—or of being deceived—which does not favor general or systematic thought. Because of this, a concern for making something coherent out of scattered pieces is almost always absent. To this must be added the pusillanimity of any critiques directed at the predominant political economy. Contemporary social thought is marked by this fragmentation, incoherence, and timidity before the institutions and power structures holding sway in the real world. Here are to be found all the important characteristics of periods of great crisis and turmoil. And this general atmosphere is favorable to wayward conceits that often have a dangerously reactionary import.

I am not trying, in these few pages, to outline a more or less encyclopedic depiction of our epoch. The intellectual tendencies which mark it are diverse and, quite fortunately, contradictory. They cannot even be summed up under the postmodernist label, which merely represents an umbrella category under which are to be found political positions, theoretical stances, and centers of interest having so little in common that the all-embracing label itself must be regarded as dubious. Meanwhile, as I intend to demonstrate succinctly, there are fields in which contemporary social cogitation has singled out new questions having nothing to do with postmodernism, especially by interesting attempts to enrich political economy through the opening of new fields of study that accord with the evolution of the capitalist system.

It is certainly not the aim of this study to comment on all these contributions. Moreover, being temperamentally predisposed not to lambaste views I find unconvincing but rather to seek out whatever is interesting, or even novel, in what they bring to the table, I will, insofar as is possible, avoid any lazy lumping together of discrepant ideas—more especially so since the viewpoints at issue are often individual ones and because theoretical stances which, in my opinion, offer support to the fashionable neoliberal utopia do not necessarily fit in with the political stances of their authors. Undoubtedly, we have seen known advocates of postmodernism show up on French television to denounce the great strike movement of November-December 1995 as "rabble rousing"— just as they are now set to denounce any refusal to submit to behests prompted by the workings of neoliberal policies. But other intellectuals, though willing to be qualified by the same adjective "postmodernist," took up less reactionary political positions and some of them even boldly challenged the neoliberal utopia.

What I intend to emphasize at this point are the strongly media-sponsored interpretations prescribed for shaping the dominant ideology, the "current intellectual fashions" whose critique is pointed to in the title of this work. Nevertheless, I will pass up the overly easy job of shooting down clumsy media-sponsored demagogies, like those of the notorious "new philosophers" who quickly went over to the traditional right and were forgotten just as quickly. Nor will I dwell on those sociological views, imitative of North

American models, which have been taken up in Europe in surprisingly uncritical fashion. This descriptive sociology, no doubt, provides some useful information about changes affecting contemporary society, including upheavals in production methods, computerization, urbanization, education, and mass-media culture. It also gives some good descriptions of the critical state of those forms of social and political organization, like democratic institutions, carried over from earlier periods. But it stops there, forbidden to raise questions about the future of the society whose daily management is all that concerns it. Thus I will not take seriously these expressions of each successive dominant mode of thought, despite the evident fact that each is guaranteed short-run success by the media publicity offered to it. I therefore will center my concern on more subtle contributions in which, as is always the case with studies seeking to be in the vanguard, it is hard to disentangle the diverse (and sometimes contradictory) import of their propositions.

The emphasis of this body of work on language, its denunciation as an instrument of the power structure, and its deconstruction has certainly opened new perspectives to social thought and must already be credited with contributions, or even discoveries, whose fertile capacity is far from being exhausted. In this regard, the names of Michel Foucault and Jacques Derrida spring to mind.

In the long series of his major works, Michel Foucault is quite convincing in his view that language is, for power structures, a medium of domination and of repression. In this sense, he has made a far from negligible contribution to a radical critical theory aiming toward human emancipation. But what I find regrettable is that he has held back from identifying the sources of and causes for the existence of these power structures. Was it because he regarded these as so obvious as to need no explanation? Or, on the contrary, is it that when one goes beyond platitudes admitting of little doubt (the power of capital in our social system), the task of proof is far more complex than one might guess, since the topic of specific forms of alienation governed by the logic specific to each power structure has scarcely been explored, in contrast to the Marxist theory of economic alienation and of the reproduction of the capitalist mode of production? (In this connection I refer to what I have written on this topic in *Eurocentrism*.) I lean toward this second explanation, and thus regret even more that Foucault, whose political stance, moreover, was always brave and hostile to the established system of dominance, was not bold enough to go further. Was it his turn to fear "falling victim to the ravages of conceptualization," a fear that, as we will see, strongly marks the thought of our epoch because this epoch is a period of crisis?

Jacques Derrida, in his most recent book *Specters of Marx* (Routledge, 1994), not only takes a firm stance against neoliberalism and the destructive capitalist offensive it signifies but also offers a bold definition of the "Marxist spirit," which he identifies with the undertaking of radical critique. I certainly have the very greatest sympathy for this definition, which emphasizes that "reason" and "liberation" are synonymous—an essential element in my own analysis.

But the problem is precisely that deconstructionism seeks protection from its greatest fear: domination by concepts and conceptual thought. In this sense it really does belong to our epoch, with its distrust of philosophy's tradition of critical thought. Its appeal to give up on any attempt to investigate the essence of things forces it to remain within the bounds of purely relative surface perceptions. To be sure, surrealism was the forerunner of this critique of language and poetic and fictional writing, as well as images and painting. But unfortunately, surrealism's revolutionary potential has by now been generally forgotten.

Jean François Lyotard, because he has been more vigorous than others in expressing distrust for conceptual thinking and for the spirit of radical critique, is in some ways the figurehead of our period's postmodernist ideology. What I wrote above on the supposed failure of modernity (which allegedly resulted in Hitler and Auschwitz), on postmodernism's rejection of so-called "great narratives," and lastly on the open abandonment of liberatory aspirations, all refer directly to the series of writings by Lyotard and to his evolution commencing with *Derive a partir de Marx et Freud* and concluding with his very slight *The Postmodern Explained: Correspondence, 1982-1985* (University of Minnesota Press, 1993).

Postmodernism is a wayward conceit expressing disconcertedness at foresight, will, and consequential action, which is distinguished by distrust for systematic thought, in the place of which it puts what Gianni Vattimo aptly terms "flaccid thought," ready to accept anything since all theories are equally [in]valid and nothing is objectively true. Of course, there is nothing novel about this attitude—it is indeed a feature to be found at all moments of great crisis. Here, likewise, Vattimo in *The End of Modernity: Nihilism and Hermeneutics in Postmodern Culture* (John Hopkins University Press, 1988) unmasks the grounds for this deviance in the clearest of terms: "The perspective of reappropriating existence, of reforming it, of escaping from the realm of exchange value and centering social life on use value, this perspective is a wreck, and not merely in terms of practical failures and bankruptcies (which would leave intact its value as an ideal and a norm). In reality the perspective of reappropriation, like God in Nietzsche, has lost even its significance as an ideal norm, it has at last been disclosed to be completely superfluous."

This abandonment of will—of the will to construct a different social order, beginning with a radical critique of the present order—results inevitably in nihilism. But this entitles us to pose another question: what crisis shows itself in this nihilism? And where is it headed?

The thesis presented here is that this crisis is entirely a crisis of capitalism: not a temporary slump or even a long structural slump, both of which would be forms of crisis within the system. Rather it is a crisis of the system in regard to its most essential feature, economic alienation. In other words, capitalism has reached a critical stage in that it has already created objective conditions which require that it be overstepped. I have already analyzed this overstepping, which nevertheless cannot come about automatically as if it were a "force of nature," in terms of the necessity of a cultural revolution based on the withering away of the law of value. My thesis that underdetermination governs the social realm (in contrast to the structuralist overdetermination thesis) signifies that we are confronted with the alternative of overstepping capitalism precisely by way "of reforming existence, by escaping from the realm of exchange value," or otherwise by treading water. These are two historical possibilities, but it must be understood that the second of them can only lead to the self-destruction of society. Rosa Luxemburg grasped this, three quarters of a century ahead of time, when she proclaimed that the choice before humanity was "socialism or barbarism." It follows from this analysis that the postmodernist option is, at bottom, to choose self-destructive nihilism. And because the starting point of postmodernism is reduction of all modernity to that form of modernity resulting from historical capitalism, for it the end of this modernity takes the place of the end of capitalism, of whose causes, forms, and symptoms postmodernism can offer no analysis.

Despite my negative evaluation of postmodernism as an ideology of crisis, of the capitulation of reason, and of reactionary abandonment of the indispensable perspective of liberation, I do not draw the conclusion that contemporary social studies as a whole, though by and large beguiled by the features of this "current intellectual fashion," are completely worthless. On the contrary, the relativism that has predominated since 1968 has, in some ways, favored a degree of progress in specific fields of social study. Many have been encouraged by it to venture off the beaten paths.

The broad field of political economy has, perhaps more than others, been favorably affected by a spirit of freedom drawn from contemporary relativism. Alongside the political economy of holistic systems, for example, studies in the sociology of innovation and in the economics of organized structures have been treated in this way. I nevertheless find it striking how impoverished are the general conclusions drawn from this work. The economics of bargaining (the French school of *l'économie des conventions* suggests a method stressing the institutional, conventional, and bargaining attitudes of social groups), for instance, is far from offering any comprehension of its topic: it is not structurally linked to the political economy of really existing capitalism, on whose challenges it sheds no light comparable to the elucidation achieved, in its time, by the theory of regulation. For example, in the field of mass psychology, so crucial to an understanding of social systems like our own, the emphasis on speculative phenomena helps, perhaps, to understand their inner workings better, but we are told nothing about the important point—why does financial speculation play such an important role in the current economic system? Grassroots historical studies are certainly not a contemporary innovation. Venerable as they are, there can be no disputing their absolute necessity. But the most current ones, in my opinion, stem from a preconception that truth is a relative, culturally defined notion. (We will return to this question, which I consider an important one.)

Meanwhile, economic science continues to be swayed by a strong leaning to mathematize. But here, too, there are nuances. Conventional macroeconomic econometrics is no novelty, dating as it does to the 1930s. It began as a technique of economic management, avoiding on principle any discussion of the social and historical bases of the economic system, and it continues to develop along the same lines. In this narrow framework, model building and dependence on mathematical and statistical methodology is obviously not merely justified but indispensable. But this is not the place for a discussion of what has recently come out of such research.

On the other hand, the mathematization of economic theory is quite another matter. This process is driven by the ambition to replace political economy as a social science (especially in its Marxist form) with a pure economics that would prove two basic propositions: that markets are self-regulating and that they lead to the best possible outcome for society. This attempt, going back to Walras in the nineteenth century, is no novelty. But despite the intensity with which it has been prosecuted ever since, it has never succeeded in proving its case. Behind the increasing sophistication of its formulations, this fruitless operation masks the emptiness of the prevailing prejudices, nothing more. Yet such dubious achievements are frequently rewarded with the Nobel Prize! Worse, this illusory theory of pure economics feeds back into the econometrics of macroeconomic management, the majority of whose models are drawn from it. It thus is no cause for astonishment that the effects promised from the neoliberal policies propounded by the master-thinkers of this mathematical economics are always belied by the facts. But, as their guru Friedrich Von Hayek would say, it is history that is wrong because it disobeys the imaginary rationality of pure economics. Conventional economists are aware of this failure, but they are taught nothing by it in regard to the status of their theory of macroeconomic management, which they tirelessly go on defending. A beneficial counterpoint to all this can be found in the devastating critique that the mathematicians Giorgio Israel and Bernard Guerrien have addressed to the blind alley signified by the mathematization of the social sciences and to the sloppiness of the mathematical techniques resorted to by the neoclassical economists.

Nevertheless, they hop right from the frying pan into the fire, lured by the hope of burying, once and for all, the rational and liberatory aspirations of social thought. In mathematics, chaos theory surely represents a new and promising branch of research, which already has allowed us to better understand some of the processes at work in various parts of the natural world (such as meteorology). I do not consider it impossible for its present discoveries to help explain operative realities in some narrowly circumscribed areas of social life, such as speculation-induced stock market fluctuations. But no one has yet shown me even a rudimentary proof that they would be of help in managing social transformations.

I find it necessary to add to these impressionistic images a warning against what I hold to be the excesses of some directions in research. A typical, and still dangerous, example is what has been called "neuronism," the search for the ultimate determinants of behavior in human biology. This is not a new sort of excess. The success of social Darwinism in the nineteenth century, and its criminal extensions in the twentieth, are notorious. On a much smaller scale, Cesare Lombroso thought that he could detect "born criminals" on the basis of their physical characteristics.

IV

Many have warned, and I share their misgivings, against the theoretical dangers involved in the prevalent state of mind by virtue of its fragmented concerns and its timorous avoidance of confrontation with the holistic functioning of the real system—dangers of new enticements to reductionism, of a false opposition between holistic and individualistic methodologies, of relativism, of culturalism—in short, of theoretical incoherence and abandonment of objectivity.

I maintain that the worst of these dangers is culturalism, because it carries with it an emphatic political stance that represents a major barrier to the shaping of democratic and working class responses to real challenges. I use the word "culturalism" to signify a double affirmation: that there are constant, transhistorical elements peculiar to each of the many human cultures; and that all of these cultures are "of equal worth." This is not a new idea: it was an unfortunate result of 1968, a bad answer to good questions posed by the rebellion against Eurocentrism. At that time Ivan Illich gave body to it, and this became the basis for his wide appeal.

Objectively, all the deficiencies of the current state of mind converge on a single point: they reinforce the neoliberal utopianism holding sway over the political economy of the contemporary phase of the crisis. Thus, in return for submission to the laws of the market in the spirit of antigovernmental right-wing anarchism, one receives promises, convincing only to those already convinced, of a convivial society, a society without enemies, a consensual society—and this is the theory of "the end of ideologies" on which this dream house is built! I agree with Cornelius Castoriadis, who sees in this climate scarcely more than "the rising tide of vacuousness" that represents one of the techniques used to manage the reality of capitalism in crisis. There is nothing more to be asked of

this capitalism in crisis: it is there, once and for all, and henceforward is exempted from what normally is obligatory for any
social order—the requirement that it establish its own legitimacy.
But in reality this is an unsustainable stance. And that is why this
neoliberal utopianism, as outlined here, is forced to cohabit with
its opposite: ethnic communalism, the spread of irrationality,
religious cultism, the rising tide of violence, and all sorts of
fanaticism. The prevailing ideology tries to get off cheaply, for
example by claiming that liberalism has merely, and temporarily,
been "polluted" by nationalism in societies, like those of Eastern
Europe, where its (always future) benefits are not yet obvious. That
argument, whose superficiality cries out (the success of capitalism
in Asia was accompanied by a strengthening of nationalism, not
its evanescence), begs the question by assuming that liberalism will
reduce the contrasts among regions of the world, even though
logical analysis of its workings proves the contrary—that it must
heighten global polarization. Or else, with even more audacity, the
claim is made, as by Jean François Lyotard, that withdrawal into
ethnic communalism is the way in which societies protect themselves from the "despotism of the idea of liberation." This is to try
to get out of trouble by a mere play on words. But behind this
lazy word play lurks severance between the concepts of reason
and liberation, clearing a highroad for the reactionary offensive
besetting our times.

The most serious thing about this is that the attitude inculcated
by postmodernism contributes gravely to curtailment of the significance of democratic practices. Mere administration of day-to-
day matters, under the constraints imposed by capitalist political
economics, leaves no scope at all for possible alternative choices.
The "low intensity democracy" resulting from this has become

extremely vulnerable, and the recrudescent appeal of various fascist movements gives grim testimony to that fact.

These disturbing developments, taken as a whole, imperil the very idea of a social theory, that is, of a coherent mental representation of society. Undoubtedly, some causal mechanisms looked to at an earlier stage of modern history have become outmoded once and for all. It is hard nowadays to believe that the inauguration of a golden age based on reason is an imminent possibility, as Enlightenment philosophers proclaimed in the eighteenth century. But is that any reason to abandon the concept of objectivity? Is it really possible to maintain, as some claim to, that the quantum theory in physics has no more claim to truth than a Jewish or Bororo cosmological creation myth, merely because the population involved (all contemporary physicists, this or that ethnic group) experience them, or used to experience them, as unquestionable realities?

My belief is that it is neither desirable nor possible to rid oneself of scientific concern: to understand, to explicate, to show how parts are linked to their wholes, how reality is made up of wholes, how parts are to be understood through the logics governing their wholes.

This being the case in the social sphere, whose reduction to the status of a natural phenomenon I consider unacceptable, the scientific spirit must be at the service of some cause, meaning that it must serve a feasible project (scientific knowledge itself, though relative and perpetually incomplete, sets the criteria for feasibility) with an explicit, undistortable, ethical purport. The alternative, social Darwinism, is not merely socially unacceptable—it is scientifically worthless.

Returning to our starting point, I maintain that we must accept risk, for freedom is worth that price. This certainly requires that we keep clear of false but reassuring teleologies, which make history into a predetermined process and mix up possibilities with imagined certainties. In this sense, criticism of the classical Enlightenment formulas and those of vulgarized historical Marxism is more than welcome, it is indispensable. My assertion of under-determination, as against overdetermination, is a proper reminder that society is not nature: there are many possibilities, and we must go from thinking in terms of necessity to thinking in terms of possibilities. "History's surprises," good or bad, by which we mean any unforeseen important events that only after the fact can be deduced from or explained by some theory, testify to the usefulness of our concept of underdetermination.

7

Communications as Ideology

The sphere of communications is one of the most important and favored subjects in contemporary social study, for which reason I have devoted this chapter to its special consideration. The viewpoints and analytic methods applied to the problems of this particular field also represent some of the most illustrative examples of the contemporary state of mind—its legitimate concerns, its silences, and its excesses.

Communication is certainly no new reality; on the contrary, it has constituted a permanent element of social life since the most distant origins of the human species. Indeed, to speak of the human race is to speak of the relations among human beings, all mediated through the acquisition and transmission (or retention) of knowledge and information by means of the rule-governed invention and use of tools for the storage and transmission of that knowledge and information. Language is the oldest and foremost among them—all forms of knowledge are conveyed in some language, and that makes all languages "vernacular" (to apply that adjective to only some languages is to indulge in ridiculous redundancy). Writing and its supporting media—mainly printing, for the last few centuries—is still the main means for the storage of knowledge and for communication. Nevertheless, it is essential to recognize that modernity, through the prodigious and accelerated development of productive forces characteristic of it, and through the mercantile-capitalist form of its underlying social relations, has so compacted the relationships among actors in economic, social, cultural, and political life that new technological supporting media have had to be invented to meet the requirements of social reproduction. Radio, telephone, photography, cinema, television, fax, computer, and the networking of systems—all are responses to these needs. As is obvious, every progressive step in this field requires resort to ever more weighty organizational and material—and hence financial—resources. Of ever increasing importance are questions relating to the cost of constructing these instruments, to the organization of access to them, and thus to their control. Accordingly, the "production" of information—its collection, selection, and transmission—has become a major claim on the whole social structure.

In this perspective, it seems that a major quantitative leap marks the cost of the communications media by which the future will be driven. "Information superhighways" are the material communications networks that must be put in place to interconnect and interact with a vast array of information, to be transmitted, stored, and used. In the current state of scientific knowledge and its technological application such "superhighways" can be built in two fashions: using broadcast satellites or fiber-optic networks. The costs, advantages, and inconveniences of each method have already been fairly well listed and calculated. It also appears that the United States has more or less chosen to give priority to the former of these methods but has been very laggard in its application, the Clinton-Gore plan in this regard having ended in near failure (Congress having refused to fund it). France, on the other hand, profiting from its earlier experiment (the Minitel network) has chosen the second solution and already possesses an extraordinary fiber-optic network of 18,600 miles set up in part by the public sector (France-Telecom, the French National Railways) and in part by the private sector (the Lyons Water Company).

Each of these technological solutions requires enormously costly investments, beyond the reach of all but rich governments and the largest multinational corporations. But much the same was already the case, *mutatis mutandis*, at the turn of the century when radio and telephone communications networks had to be put in place, and again more recently with networks to provide television coverage.

The battle to control these instrumentalities unrolls in two dimensions, one largely national, the other global.

At the level of nations (or sometimes groups of closely linked states, as is hoped for the European Union) this is the choice: assuming that the production and storage of information is roughly free (that is to say, uncensored except by their required costs, and notably their capital cost), should its transmission be undertaken by a public service (like the post office), by private businesses, or by some combination, still to be worked out, of the two sectors? Should this transmission be as free as possible, or should it be subject to criteria (of an ethical, political, or other nature) that are still to be worked out? The weight of the current mental outlook, of course, is rather favorable to free market solutions. Information would thus be treated as a commodity and its transmission would be a commercial service, governed by the laws of the market. The market, then, would determine who can have access to it based on ability to pay the market price for the commodity and for the service. Choosing consumers by their wallets will determine what items of knowledge and information are worth gathering (those which are salable) and which are not. Public service criteria, on the other hand, might modify the make-up of the mass of consumers, distribute the cost burden differently, and work according to standards that would assure more equality (or less inequality) of access and more democratic (more objective, more pluralist, etc.) conditions of use.

The stakes are so great that great multinational corporations look to them as the major source of their future financial profitability. Already, economic activities classified under the headings of digital technology, telecommunications, and audiovisual media account for eight to ten percent of the world's gross industrial production, more than the automobile industry. This proportion will increase, and quickly, since three out of five wage earners in the world already make use of digital technology. However, until now the field of communication remains broadly (though there are big differences among countries) subject to legal regulation and is administered as a public service. The offensive of private capital, summoning up for this purpose its preferred and well-known themes (like the efficiency of private enterprise) is simply aiming at deregulation, which would allow it to get its hands on the juicy profits in prospect.

On the global scale, the question is whether national boundaries need to be wiped out to permit private, and on occasion public, capitalist firms to extend their operations over the whole world, or whether states are to insist on senior partnership in this domain. The solution advocated by the predominant political and ideological tendencies, globalized deregulation, would surely have devastating consequences for most of the world's countries (indeed, for the whole world beyond the United States, Canada, the European Union, and Japan). For outside those metropolitan countries and the private capitalist groups based in them, there is not a single national state capable of competing on a level playing field with the U.S., European, and Japanese multinationals. Yet the market on which they focus their concerns comprises scarcely more than that twenty percent of the world's population (a majority in the metropolitan centers, a minority in rapidly growing peripheral countries, a mere handful in the marginalized remainder), accounting for eighty percent of the world's consumer purchases. Precisely for that reason I have included this monopoly over information and communication among the "five monopolies" through which global polarization can be expected, in conformity with the logic of global capitalist development to intensify rather than diminish for the foreseeable future.

But worse is yet to come. Even assuming that, in metropolitan centers and peripheral countries alike, the public service option comes to prevail in the organization of the market (in such case pseudo-market) for information and its transmission, that would represent no guarantee of any correction to global imbalances. In peripheral countries, the public services which, there also, would be assigned the task of administering communications media would still be deprived of resources. The private, and even the public service, corporations of the metropolitan centers would act together to batten these fragile peripheral fields and draw juicy profits from them. In this respect, as in others, there is no way to effectively combat the natural tendency of globalized capitalism to produce, replicate, and deepen polarization except by the organization of interdependence under negotiated rules. This would involve systematic and concerted action in all spheres, and in particular the organization of capital transfers, destined to the construction of necessary infrastructure, from metropolitan to peripheral countries. I will not here go into these questions, which

I have taken up elsewhere in detail, nor into the answers that would comprise the political economy of a polycentric globalized system that would accomplish a steady diminution of global polarization, and consequently lay the groundwork for a sustained development that would be both popular and democratic.

Now, any discussion of these real interests has been completely emptied out of the prevalent discourse on "communications," thanks to the fact that all tendencies in the predominant school of social thought have gone over to the theories propounded in the political economy of globalized neoliberalism, and thanks to the docile submission of postmodernists, neomodernists, et al., to the exactions of that political economy. Thus, in place of a debate over these true stakes, we have a purely ideological discourse, which Philippe Breton quite properly terms "communications utopianism."

In this utopian discourse, the word "communications" has come to mean just about anything and, consequently, has become meaningless. "Communication" is spoken of without ever referring to its content, to what it is that is being communicated—communication as an end in itself! The human being is said to have become *homo communicans*, as if it ever had been anything else. But behind that label lurks a certain concept of this human as an other-directed individual who merely reacts to the messages assailing it but is incapable of self-direction prompted by its own inner workings—in other words, incapable of action in the true meaning of the verb "to act." In short, Madison Avenue's ideal consumer! So drastic a depreciation of human nature courts a fantastical excess: human beings having themselves become machines (computers), confusion between what is alive and what is artificial becomes obligatory almost as a matter of course. (Intelligent machines can be built, and in truth, they are at least as intelligent as these ideal idiots.)

Accordingly, from the silences within this discourse we can extract the main question: what forms of knowledge, what sorts of information, for whom and to what end? Undoubtedly, the mass of knowledge and information needed for contemporary social and economic life is much greater than what was needed in the distant past, or even in the recent past. The fact remains that we still need to distinguish between knowledge and information. We can be flooded by an excess of insignificant data and, under their impact, lose that capacity to analyze and to understand without which there is no knowledge. Media manipulators are well aware of these methods and know perfectly well how to use them. A vast array of data on stock-market transactions might seem useful to a speculator (though I regard this as most dubious), but what is its social utility?

In our mercantile world, there is great risk that priority will go to the collection and sale of data that will be useful for market management according to the narrow outlook of the biggest corporations (the major multinationals) for whom the right "just in time" decisions on markets and production can bring in substantial profits. In the same way, other possibilities opened by the powers of modern communications technology are considered only as they pertain to dominant commercial interests. For example, decentralization of the labor process (telecommuting, as practiced by many airlines, banks, insurance companies, and even law offices) has already been pressed into service on behalf of wage-reduction policies.

Technological progress and the invention of new technologies are certainly still desirable in themselves (I am not one of those who are inspired by nostalgia for the past and its rustic conviviality); but the distinction between instruments and the uses to which they are put remains an essential one. The naive beliefs of Marshall

McLuhan notwithstanding, history does not unfold in a manner
directly governed by technological progress. History, rather, is a
matter of struggle for control over the way in which these technologies are to be used, and this, at bottom, is an aspect of struggles
within society, including class struggles and national struggles.
Thus, the conditions that will favor utilization of technology on
behalf of social progress, for the liberation of individuals and
peoples, have to be created. Most fortunately, such conditions exist
and are operative, often not in accordance with the wishes of the
system's dominant forces. It was once said that the telephone was
invented to allow people to go to the opera without leaving home.
The public took it over to do many other things. As we know, the
Minitel likewise was, for better or worse, taken over by the public.
It once was hard to see what usefulness a facsimile machine might
have, and for that reason the perfection of the invention was long
delayed. We know how that turned out. The success of these
particular devices should strengthen our optimism: people, as
users, can acquire mastery of their instruments and put them to
use for their chosen strategies in their chosen arenas. However,
though in the case of some particular media knowledge has been
gained without organized intervention, this is not the case for
other instruments of communication, for whose appropriate usage
a collective, strongly organized, and political battle will be required: putting television at the service of democracy is a fine
example. In the same way, the organization of popular access to
information superhighways, and the imposition on a national and
world scale of an acceptable and socially useful allocation of their
services, are also at stake in battles still to be fought.

   Through its silence on conflicts of interest—justified by the
inane presumption (often explicit in professedly postmodern writings) that a pacified, conflictless, consensus-based social order is

just around the corner—communications-utopian discourse serves to disarm peoples and nations, forcing them to accept deregulation for the benefit of the multinationals. This is often done on the ground that "there is no alternative" (a slogan used to rationalize just about anything, and especially submission to the supposed constraints of the market).

Communications utopianism is not a new ideology. It has been a constant feature of the social thought prevalent for the whole postwar period, even though the rapidly succeeding waves of fashion that mark the contemporary world put it on stage only occasionally. It is not to be forgotten that in the 1940s and 1950s cybernetics nourished the discourse (and the illusions) then prevalent. The American school of cybernetics (Wiener & Co.) thought that it had discovered, in the apparatus of mathematics, a common denominator governing all natural and social laws (yet another case of this mix up). This supposed discovery of laws ordering the relationships among all elements of the cosmos ("communications") would obviously allow the overstepping of conflict-based ideologies, would allow creation of a perfectly adapted new man freed from any need to rebel and with no inner life, manipulable. An old formulation of the contemporary discourse. Forgotten in as brief a time as that during which it was headlined by the dominant media, cybernetics gave way in the 1960s and 1970s to the supposed digital revolution, which, in its turn, was supposed to undergird democracy by simply generalizing the use of computers, thus allowing each citizen-consumer to make all choices (from shopping at the supermarket to voting in elections) as intelligently as possible! Isn't it the case that, in at least one of its aspects, contemporary discourse on information highways is nothing more than a reversion to those simple-minded utterances?

There certainly is nothing unreal about the instruments of digital technology or about the amplification, through interconnected networks, of the intensity with which they are utilized. But once again, these powerful instruments, by themselves, cannot give rise to any specific sort, whether paradisiacal or nightmarish, of social order. They are objects of a struggle that will tell how they will fit into alternative, but equally possible, visions of the future.

8

Pure Economics, or the Contemporary World's Witchcraft

In all the universities of the contemporary world an odd sort of subject is taught called economic science, or simply economics, as one might say "physics." It would take as its field of study the economic life of a society, with the aspiration of scientifically explaining its crucial magnitudes such as prices, wages, incomes, rates of interest, foreign exchange rates, and total unemployment.

However, and this fact is strange indeed, while scientific research takes reality as its point of departure, economics is based on a resolutely anti-realistic founding principle. This principle, called "methodological individualism," treats society as nothing more than the aggregate of its component individuals, each of which, as *Homo oeconomicus*, is in turn defined in terms of laws expressing what, for it, would be rational behavior. It is left rather unclear whether, in the outlook of this "science," the mental structure built on the basis of interaction among these behaviors is supposed to give us a picture approximating social reality, or whether it is put forward normatively, as a model of an ideal social order.

It is a platitude, undeniable as such, that individuals are the basic elements of any society. But what reason is there not to take into account that real society, far from being built up out of direct encounters among individual behaviors, is an infinitely more complex structure combining social classes, nations, states, big businesses, collective projects, and political and ideological forces. Economists take no notice of these obvious realities, because they are hindrances to constructing a "pure economics" and revealing its fundamental laws, meaning the laws which would follow from an economic structure stripped of any social dimension except the interaction of purely individual projects and activities. It might at best, perhaps, be an enjoyable mental game to make up this pure economics, but is it at all related to reality? Luckily for our health, doctors have not made up a "pure medicine" after the fashion of "pure economics." Can one imagine a medical science which models the workings of the human body on the exclusive basis of cells, taken to be the only fundamental elements of the human body, while deliberately taking no notice of bodily organs like the heart or liver? It is about as likely that the most complex model, if restricted to interactions among cells, would produce anything resembling a human body as it is that the random pecking of a pigeon at a keyboard would produce the complete works of Shakespeare! The same goes for the likelihood of reaching a general equilibrium—and an optimal one no less—by virtue of market encounters among five billion human beings.

Taking this absurd starting point as a legitimate one leads to bizarre paraphilosophical effusions. Friedrich Von Hayek, who our neoliberal economists take as their guru, could not refuse to admit the existence of nations, national states, social classes, and a few other aspects of reality, but he was quite content to dismiss them as "irrational" residues. He thus was glad to set up a mythical rationality in place of the search for rational explication of reality.

A human being certainly belongs to the class of rational animals, and its behaviors, even the oddest among them, can probably be comprehended. But only on the condition that the particular rational processes motivating human actions be placed in an appropriate framework to specify contextually their scope and their mechanisms. In other words, a holistic stance, which bases its reasoning on real totalities (firms, classes, states), is the only attitude from which science can proceed. Classical political economy (and the adjective "political" was not there by chance) as practiced by Smith, Ricardo, Marx, and Keynes, adopted this scientific attitude as a matter of course.

Furthermore, as an intelligent animal, a human being modifies its behavior to take account of the responses it expects from others. Accordingly, the models of pure economics ought to be based on the rationality requirements not of a simple-minded and immediate response (price comes down—I buy more), but of a response mediated by expectations of other people's responses (I'll postpone my purchases if I think the price will go down even further). Is a model comprising all these individual subjective data even possible? And if so, would it go to the heart of the problem or would it be beside the point?

Pure economics starts off with musings about the behavior of Robinson Crusoe on his island, choosing between consuming now and storing up for the future. But its "Robinsonisms" go further. So these economists picture the world as made up of five billion Crusoes. Their textbooks start with a bizarre opening chapter in which these five billion elemental units are presented as "pure consumers," each initially endowed with its own "asset basket," each resorting to a perfectly competitive market to get things it wishes to have in exchange for possessions superfluous to its needs.

This style is manifestly that of a fable, attributing to its animal characters a humanly plausible pattern of behavior in order to reach a typified outcome, the "moral of the story." Our pure economics is like that. At each stage in the unfolding of its narrative it resorts to whatever plausible assumption about behavior will lead to its predetermined conclusion.

The conundrum ensuing directly from the choice of methodological individualism is this: how can it be proven that interaction among the rational behaviors of many individuals, each of which involves expectations about all other behaviors, will lead to a determinate equilibrium—i.e., a system characterized by one, and only one, set of prices, incomes, and unemployment and growth rates? Obviously, this is a matter for mathematical techniques.

But this is precisely what mathematics proves is not, in general, the case. This sort of system of simultaneous equations (and we are dealing here with hundreds of billions of equations) tends strongly, *a priori*, to be inconsistent—thus, yielding no solution. With a sufficiently large number of additional assumptions it may, just possibly, become consistent but indeterminate (yielding an infinite number of solutions), and with a yet much larger number of additional assumptions might be made determinate (yielding but one solution).

Practitioners of pure economics, accordingly, have the task of finding just the right set of assumptions to reach their goal. With that criterion in mind, they decide that some functions aggregating behaviors display as convex curves and others as concave, that some production functions exhibit diminishing returns and others constant or increasing returns. And each step in their demonstration will be bolstered by a suitable fable.

The Arrow-Debreu model, that feather in the cap of pure economics, does indeed prove that, once all the needed assumptions have been made—and, moreover, the system as a whole has been assumed to be *perfectly* competitive—there exists at least one solution yielding general equilibrium. However, system-wide perfect competition notoriously presumes the existence of a universal auctioneer to consolidate and publicize all offers to buy and to sell. Thus, oddly enough, this model demonstrates that a central planner, with perfect knowledge of the behavioral possibilities of each of his five billion clients, would make all the decisions needed to produce the sought-after equilibrium! The model does not demonstrate that really existing free markets can produce it. At least we can get a moment's amusement from the fact that the pure economics favored by neoliberal extremists must fall back on Big Brother to solve its problems! Obviously, absent the auctioneer, the system is constantly changing in accord with the results of the real behavior of individuals in the course of their marketplace transactions. Equilibrium, if it were ever to be reached, would be as much the result of trial and error, of gropings—a matter of chance—as of rational factors in the behavior of those active in the marketplace. Such an equilibrium will never, in all probability, exist. Moreover, Sonnenschein's theorem proves the impossibility of deducing the form of supply and demand functions from functions specifying the maximizing behavior of the individuals. But what does it matter to pure economics that serious mathematicians prove it to be stuck in a blind alley? As we will see, a very different question is at issue.

Moreover, even assuming the miracle that it would take for general equilibrium to result from marketplace encounters among buyers and sellers, such an equilibrium would lack essential characteristics—it would specify no particular rate of unemployment, no particular growth rate for output. True enough, unemployment is no concern of pure economics, which presumes a world in which all unemployment is voluntary! This definitional presumption being obviously false, conventional economists accompany their absurd discourse about the achievement of equilibrium merely through the workings of (supposedly self-regulating) markets with another dose of nonsense about unemployment, which they arbitrarily, and with trite reactionary prejudice, attribute to wages being "too high." In doing so they arrogantly close their eyes not only to the fact that demand depends to a substantial degree on wages, but also to the very logic of their own system, in which any change in wages alters all the data relevant to the system of general equilibrium.

Next comes the claim that such a general equilibrium would also represent a "social optimum." This affirmation is the second of pure economics's great propositions. But in this case the "proof" rests on a meaningless definition of optimality—as the quality of an equilibrium none of whose parameters can be changed, even in the slightest, without making at least one individual worse off. In other words, an equilibrium condemning four billion to stagnant poverty would still be "optimal," so long as it could not be altered without costing even a penny to the richest billionaire among the five billion inhabitants of our planet!

This splendid structure of pure economics, first envisioned—obviously in response to Marxist analysis—toward the close of the nineteenth century, systematically disregarded money, which was regarded as merely a veil obscuring the real economy. But since, all the same, money does exist, the time came when it had to be given a place in that structure. The only acceptable way was to adopt the most simple-minded form of the quantity theory. In the wake of this move, monetarism—the latest style in pure economics—by decreeing that money was just one more commodity, authorized the addition of five billion individuals' demand schedules for money to their supply and demand schedules for other commodities. As for the money supply, it is to be treated as an exogenous variable determined by a central bank. An elementary scientific analysis of money creation proves that money is not a commodity like the others, because its supply is determined by the demand for it, which in turn depends partly on interest rates and partly on the level of business activity. Moreover, central banks, which are supposed to administer the money supply, which they have magical powers to set, in a neutral and independent (of whom?) fashion, do not, because they cannot, accomplish any such thing. Their action merely has a partial and indirect effect on the demand for money through their choices about interest rates.

But what is left out is that these choices react back upon the level of business activity (through the timing of investment and consumption decisions) and thus alter all the data affecting equilibrium levels. By rejecting any holistic analysis, and thus ignoring the distinction, useful in this context, between the logic of purely financial strategies and the logic of productive investment strategies, monetarist pure economics finds itself barred from investigating the real causes and factors determining interest rates.

That such an absurd and sterile exercise as pure economics should be an object of interest to normally intelligent individuals is something to be wondered at. If anyone had set out to prove that, in the field of social thought, a desperate effort to validate vested ideologies, prejudices, and interests would extinguish any scientific or critical state of mind, he could have done no better than to invent pure economics.

Pure economics is claimed to be a science on the same level as physics. That is scarcely the case, because such a claim denies the specific differentia between social and natural sciences. It is blind to the fact that society produces itself rather than being manufactured by external forces. However, it belies its own methodological principles by accepting the concept of expectations—a concept which proves that the individual, supposed to be an objective reality, is really itself an active maker of its own history.

Pure economics is a parascience. It compares to social science as parapsychology compares to psychology. Like any parascience, it can be used to demonstrate anything and its opposite. "Tell me what you want, and I will make you a model to justify it." Be it desired to raise an interest rate from 6.32 percent to 8.45 percent, to cut it to 4.26 percent, or to leave it unchanged, at hand will be an ad hoc justification disguised as an economic model. Therein lies the strength of pure economics: it is a tool in the hands of the dominant capitalists, a screen behind which they can hide their actual objectives. Currently, those objectives are to worsen unemployment and to skew the distribution of incomes still further toward the rich. Since these real aims are unavowable, it becomes useful to "prove" that they are transitional measures leading to economic growth, full employment, and jam tomorrow, as the Red Queen promised Alice.

Because it is unscientific, economics can enroll amateur mathematicians in its service just as parapsychology enrolls some psychologists. Because it doesn't matter whether or not what it proves to be the case is actually true—what counts is to validate whatever theory is being put forward—it likewise doesn't matter whether or not the "proof" is mathematically valid. Indeed, it ought to be considered bizarre that this "science" gives employment to so many incompetent mathematicians who could never hold down a job in a physics lab. There are certainly exceptions, like Debreu. But the exceptions are quick to jump out of this particular frying pan.

Leaving stereotyped pure economics behind, they go on to game theory, which analyzes encounters among strategies in which the expected reaction of other participants plays an important role. This theory certainly has substantial intellectual interest, and it furthermore can lead to progress in mathematical technique. Still, I find it striking that at every step game theory progresses further away from social reality. The same goes for the shift of attention toward chaos theory. In both cases, any social object of study serves merely as a pretext. The real aim is enrichment of mathematical theory, which is not only a legitimate objective but, even more so, is one that is essential for further progress of knowledge in many fields. Other mathematicians—like Bernard Guerrien and Giorgio Israel—have performed, precisely because they are not amateurish, the indispensable service of proving mathematically how absurd and inconsistent is the theory of pure economics.

In contrast to these exceptions is silhouetted an army of model builders, usually American college teachers, whose career hopes depend on their number of published articles which, in general, are both trivial and meaningless. Within the ruling class, pure economics is flattering to the natural inclinations of engineers and technocrats who believe, usually sincerely, that their power is unlimited and that it is their decisions which produce social reality.

The comparison with magic and witchcraft is inescapable. A wizard, likewise, dresses up his assertions in a seemingly "scientific" phraseology. He gains conviction by including some sensible and plausible things in his discourse, but only to bolster conclusions which follow from them in no way whatever. In other societies, far removed in time from ours, the magician-wizard held the spotlight. The foremost wizard was always intelligent enough to know what the king expected of him, and he delivered the goods. Pure economics performs similar functions in our economically alienated society; moreover, it performs them through similar methods, notably by an esoteric terminology (using mathematical terms to throw dust in the eyes of non-mathematicians).

Milton Friedman is the wizard-in-chief of our contemporary Oz. He understood what they wanted to hear: that wages are always too high (even in Bangladesh), that profits are still not high enough to offer the affluent sufficient investment incentives, and so on. Hence his success, despite his muddleheadedness (he might say anything, and then its opposite, depending on who is listening and when) and his proven intellectual dishonesty. Those are the very qualities sought in a wizard-in-chief, worthy of a Nobel Prize.

Moreover, as in witchcraft, cultism flourishes. Lesser wizards cluster around their pundits, each of whom furthers the careers of his own devotees. I see a similarity, indicative of this aspect of current intellectual fashions, between the proliferation of sects among economists and that among organized cults in parascience-parapsychology.

The great statesman uses "pure" economists for his own purposes, just as a great king of old chose his own agreeable wizard. Lesser politicians believe in pure economics, and the most mediocre among them, who often believe in parapsychology as well, even belong to one of pure economics' sects.

There is more to be learned about actual society and its economic structure in the shabbiest version of functionalist sociology or of vulgar Marxism than in the whole inventory of models on the shelves of pure economics. Granted that social theories must continually be kept under a critical spotlight; that the necessity of attending to what is new in social reality and to the consequent theoretical revisions is ever-present; that this discussion must always be open, free, without preconceptions—there is one thing of which I am sure, namely that anyone who follows the path of pure economics is headed straight for a dead end. That path is a blind alley precisely because pure economics is conceived as totally ahistorical, blind to every past or present dimension of social reality, blind to all possibilities of future evolution. It recognizes only "the individual," and as such it is the "pure" fruit of the crudest, most vulgar aspects of bourgeois ideology. Its preferred fable is of Crusoe on his island—the timeless, placeless, individual human. It is separated from from the scientific spirit by a full 180 degrees. As to how society reproduces itself and is the ground for its own changes, it is certainly not by obsession with the interplay among individuals that better answers to these questions are to be found.

To the bourgeois economics of his day Marx aptly applied the adjective "vulgar." It, and, a fortiori, its distillation "pure economics"—which is wrongfully termed "neoclassical" by its acolytes—is exclusively based on a single preoccupation, a preoccupation with showing that "the market" rules with the force of natural law, producing not merely a "general equilibrium" but the best of all possible equilibria, guaranteeing full employment in freedom, the "social optimum." And this preoccupation is nothing but the expression of a fundamental ideological need, the need to legitimize capitalism by making it synonymous with rationality—which, in conformity with bourgeois ideology, is seen as nothing more than the use of technically rational means for the individual pursuit of mercantile profit. On these dubious footings capitalism can be proclaimed "eternal" and be portrayed as "the end of history." Of course, economics has not merely failed to establish its basic propositions with even the most minimal scientific rigor; it has been proven methodologically incapable of ever doing so. But what's the difference? The discourse of pure economics has no real aim other than to legitimize the unrestricted predations of capital.

In contrast to this unscientific discourse, Marxian political economy, in its historical materialist method, is free from any preconception requiring it to justify this real ("real" here is to be taken as synonymous with "actual," not "rational") capitalist world. It is Marxian political economy that confronts us with the real questions: How at every moment are the "equilibria" currently marking the capitalist system determined by the class struggle—not only the basic class struggle between labor and capital, but also conflicts within the ruling class that set financial lenders against productive investors, entrepreneurs against owners, and oligopolists against each other? How do state interventions in fulfillment of the political and social logic of the dominant historical coalition (alliances among hegemonic classes and social compromises), taken together, determine the conditions of possible equilibria—notably between Department I (production of means of production) and Department II (production of means of consumption), or between these two departments and Department III (surplus-absorption)? How do they determine the level of employment (not presumed, *a priori*, to be "full") or the structure of relative prices and rents? Or the structure of interest rates? Or the pressures from above or below on the general level of prices? Or the seeming competitive advantages that govern competitiveness on world markets? Marxism puts forward no prior assumptions attributing to the system any tendency toward equilibrium. It does not hold that class struggles upset any really existing equilibrium, or even a really existing, yet provisional, disequilibrium. In sum, Marxist political economy is realistic—whereas there is no realism at all about pure economics, which abstracts from reality (classes, states, the global system) so that its discourse, emptied of reality, is left a mythical fable.

In the history of social thought, pure economics is seldom to be found center stage. To the contrary, it is usually confined to a few academic nuthouses whilst the social and political world disdainfully ignores it except for occasionally lifting, when that serves their purposes, one or another of its "conclusions" or "theses." What is required for this reactionary utopia to be put in front of the footlights, as has happened in our times, is that a set of exceptional circumstances prevail, and that all balances of social forces be overturned, leaving capital on top and unconstrained. This set of extraordinary circumstances must be very temporary, if only because, contrary to what is claimed by that reactionary utopianism (a claim that can be summed up in one sentence: maximal, unrestrained, unlimited free enterprise will, all by itself, guarantee the most wonderful possible social progress!), the un-constrained domination of capital can result in nothing but a profound social crisis. Pure economics may appear to be an excellent tool for crisis management from the perspective of the capitalist group that gains from prolongation of the crisis (currently the globalized financial markets), but a way out of the crisis it certainly is not. If society is ever to emerge from its crisis, that can only come about through the establishment of a new balance of social forces—to be produced by the class struggle—in which classes, nations, nation-states, and firms (in other words, all the realities to which pure economics is blind) will find their appropriate places. Then pure economics will be sent back to its academic asylums, not to be heard from again.

Bibliography

Alexander, Jeffrey C. *Fin de Siècle Social Theory: Relativism, Reduction, and the Problem of Reason.* New York: Verso, 1995.

Amin, Samir. *Capitalism in the Age of Globalization: The Management of Contemporary Society.* London: Zed, 1996.

———. *Les défis de la mondialisation.* Paris: L'Harmattan, 1996. Chapter 4 and 5.

———. *L'Ethnie à l'assaut des Nations.* Paris: L'Harmattan, 1994.

———. *Eurocentrism.* Translated by Russell Moore. New York: Monthly Review Press, 1989.

———. *La gestion capitaliste de la crise.* Paris: L'Harmattan, 1995.

———. *Mondialisation et Accumulation.* Paris: L'Harmattan, 1993.

———. *Re-Reading the Postwar Period: An Intellectual Itinerary.* Translated by Michael Wolfers. New York: Monthly Review Press, 1994: pp. 47-78, 169-213.

Arrighi, Giovanni. "Marxist Century—American Century: The Making and Remaking of the World Labor Movement" in *Transforming the Revolution: Social Movements and the World-System.* Edited by Samir Amin, Giovanni Arrighi, Andre Gunder Frank, Immanuel Wallerstein. New York: Monthly Review Press, 1990: pp. 54-95.

Baudrillard, Jean. *For a Critique of the Political Economy of the Sign.* Translated by Charles Levin. St. Louis: Telos, 1981.

Beaud, Michel. *Technosciences et dynamiques économiques mondiales, sur l'émergence d'un capitalisme post-industriel.* Unpublished, untranslated.

Breton, Philippe. *L'utopie de la communication.* Paris: La Découverte, 1995.

Castoriadis, Cornelius. *La montée de l'insignifiance.* Paris: Le Seuil, 1994.

Derrida, Jacques. *Du droit à la Philosophie.* Paris: Galilée, 1990.

—. *Points...: Interviews, 1974-1994.* Edited by Elisabeth Weber. Translated by Peggy Kamuf [et. Al]. Stanford: Stanford University Press, 1995.

—. *Positions.* Translated by Alan Bass. Chicago: University of Chicago Press, 1981.

—. *Specters of Marx.* Translated by Peggy Kamuf. New York: Routledge, 1994.

—. *Writing and Difference.* Translated by Alan Bass. Chicago: University of Chicago Press, 1978.

Dosse, François. *The Empire of Sense.* Forthcoming from University of Minnesota Press, 1998.

Foucault, Michel. *The Archaeology of Knowledge.* Translated by A. M. Sheridan Smith. New York: Pantheon Books, 1982.

—. *Discipline and Punish: The Birth of the Prison.* Translated by A. M Sheridan Smith. New York: Vintage Books, 1979.

—. *The Discourse on Language.* Translated by A. M. Sheridan Smith. New York: Pantheon Books, 1972.

—. *Madness and Civilization: A History of Insanity in the Age of Reason.* Translated by Richard Howard. New York: Pantheon Books, 1965.

—. *The Order of Things: An Archaeology of the Human Sciences.* Translated by A. M. Sheridan Smith. New York: Pantheon, 1970.

—. *Résumé des Cours 1970-1982.* Paris: Julliard, 1989.

Gorz, André. *Paths to Paradise: On the Liberation From Work.* Translated by Malcolm Imrie. Boston: South End Press, 1985.

Guerrien, Bernard. *Dictionnaire d'analyse économique.* Paris: Repères, 1996.

—. *L'économie néo-classique.* Paris: La Découverte, 1996.

Hochraich, Diana. *Les pays d'Asie et le marché mondial.* Unpublished manuscript.

In Defense of History: Marxism and the Postmodern Agenda. Edited by Ellen Meiksins Wood and John Bellamy Foster. New York: Monthly Review Press, 1997.

Ingrao, Bruna and Giorgio Israël. *The Invisible Hand: Economic Equilibrium in the History of Science.* Translated by Ian McGilvray. Cambridge: MIT Press, 1990.

Israël, Giorgio. "Mathematical Economics," in *Companion Encyclopedia of the History and Philosophy of the Mathematical Sciences.* 2 Vols., Edited by I. Grattan-Guinness. London, New York: Routledge, 1994.

—. *La Mathématisation du Réel.* Paris: Le Seuil, 1996.

Kremer-Marietti, Angèle. *Michel Foucault.* Paris: Livre de Poche, 1985.

Latouche, Serge. *The Westernization of the World: The Significance, Scope, and Limits of the Drive Towards Global Uniformity.* Translated by Rosemary Morris. Malden, Massachusetts: Polity Press, 1996.

Lipietz, Alain. *La Société en Sablier.* Paris: La Découverte, 1996.

Lyotard, Jean François. *Dérive à partir de Marx et Freud*. Paris: Union générale d'éditions, 1973.

—. *The Differend: Phrases in Dispute*. Translated by Georges Van Den Abbeele. Minneapolis: University of Minnesota Press, 1988.

—. *Les immatériaux*. Paris: Centre Pompidou, 1985.

—. *The Postmodern Codition: A Report on Knowledge*. Translated Geoff Bennington and Brian Massumi. Minneapolis: University of Minnesota Press, 1984.

—. *The Postmodern Explained: Correspondence, 1982-1985*. Edited by Julian Pefanis and Morgan Thomas. Translated by Don Barry [et. al]. Minneapolis: University of Minnesota Press, 1993.

Malinvaud, Edmond. *Voies de la recherche macro-économique*. Paris: Odile Jacob, 1991.

Ménard, Claude. *L'économie des organisations*. Repères, La Découverte 1995.

Mills, C. Wright. *The Sociological Imagination*. New York: Oxford Press, 1959.

Prigogine, Ilya. *Les lois du chaos*. Paris: Flammarion, 1994.

Prigogine, Ilya and Isabelle Stenghers. *La nouvelle alliance*. Paris: Gallimard, 1979.

Ruby, Christian. *Histoire de la Philosophie*. Paris: Repères, 1991.

—. *Introduction à la Philosophie politique*. Paris: Repères, 1996.

Sebai, Farida and Carlos Vercellone. *Réduction du Temps de Travail et Revenue Citoyenneté*. Futur Antérieur, 1996.

Sève, Lucien. *Critique de Lyotard*. Révolution.

Touraine, Alain. *Critique of Modernity*. Translated by David Macey. Cambridge: Blackwell, 1995.

—. *The Self-Production of Society*. Translated by Derek Coltman. Chicago: University of Chicago Press, 1977.

Vattimo, Gianni. *The End of Modernity: Nihilism and Hermeneutics in Postmodern Culture (Parallax: Re-Visions of Culture and Society)*. Translated by Jon R. Snyder. Baltimore: Johns Hopkins University Press, 1988.

Virilio, Paul. *Pure War*. Translated by Mark Polizzotti. New York: Semiotext(e), 1997.

—*Speed and Politics: An Essay on Dromology*. Translated by Mark Polizzotti. New York: Semiotext(e), 1988.

Wieviorka, Michel. *La démocratie à l'épreuve*. Paris: La Découverte, 1983.

Wilke, Joachim. *Les tourments de la raison*. Paris: L'Harmattan, 1997.

Yoshihara, Kunio. *The Rise of Ersatz Capitalism in South-East Asia*. Singapore; New York: Oxford University Press, 1988.

Zeiten, Andere. *PDS Statement Issued by the Crossover Conference*. Sozialistische Politik und Wirtshaft, Utopie *Kreativ* Berlin, 1996.

Zima, Pierre V. *La déconstruction*. Paris: Presses Universitaires de France, 1994.

Index